Simatai Great Wall
司马台长城

Jiankou Great Wall
箭扣长城

Snow-covered landscape of Bada Ridge Great Wall

八达岭长城雪景

THE ETERNAL GREAT WALL

永远的长城

图书在版编目（CIP）数据

永远的长城／旅舜 杨茵编. —北京：中国民族摄影艺术出版社，2005.1
ISBN 7-80069-644-8

Ⅰ.长... Ⅱ.旅... Ⅲ.长城—旅游画册 Ⅳ.K928.77-64

中国版本图书馆CIP数据核字（2004）第125115号

Planner: Lu Shun	策　划：旅　舜
Editor-in-Chief: Yang Yin	主　编：杨　茵
Managing Editor: Lu Baochun	责任编辑：鲁宝春
Executive Editor: Li Jiang	执行编辑：李　江
Chinese Writer: Dong Yaohui	中文撰稿：董耀会
Photographers: Zhang Zhaoji Tan Ming Bian Zhiwu Yang Yin Jiang Jingyu Li Jiang	摄　影：张肇基　谭　明　卞志武　杨　茵　姜景余
Wang Wenbo Wu Jianhua Zhang Zhenguang Wu Jiping Li Tongxi	李　江　王文波　吴健骅　张振光　武冀平
Zheng Yan Zhao Shaojun Hou Zongxiang	李同喜　郑　严　赵绍君　侯宗祥
(Some of photographs offered by the China Great Wall Society)	（部分图片由中国长城学会提供）
Translator: Tan Baoquan	翻　译：谭宝泉
Designing Producer: Zhao Hongsheng	设计制作：赵鸿生

The Eternal Great Wall

Published by China Nationality Art Photograph Publishing House

Produced by Beijing Hua Tian International Tourism Advertising Company

Book Size: 889 × 1194 (mm)　1/12

Printed Sheet: 13　　　Print Number: 1-3,000

Edition: the 1st Printing of the 1st Edition, February 2005

Edition: the 1st Printing of the Revised Edition, January 2008

ISBN 7-80069-644-8/J · 400

Telephone: 010-67118480　13910734033

http://www.jdbybook.com　http://www.旅游图书.cn

《永远的长城》

中国民族摄影艺术出版社　出版

北京华天旅游国际广告公司　承制

开本：889 × 1194 （mm）1/12

印张：13　印数：1-3000

版次：2005年2月第一版第一次印刷

版次：2008年1月修订版第一次印刷

书号：ISBN 7-80069-644-8/J · 400

电话：010-67118480　13910734033

http://www.jdbybook.com　http://www.旅游图书.cn

00018000

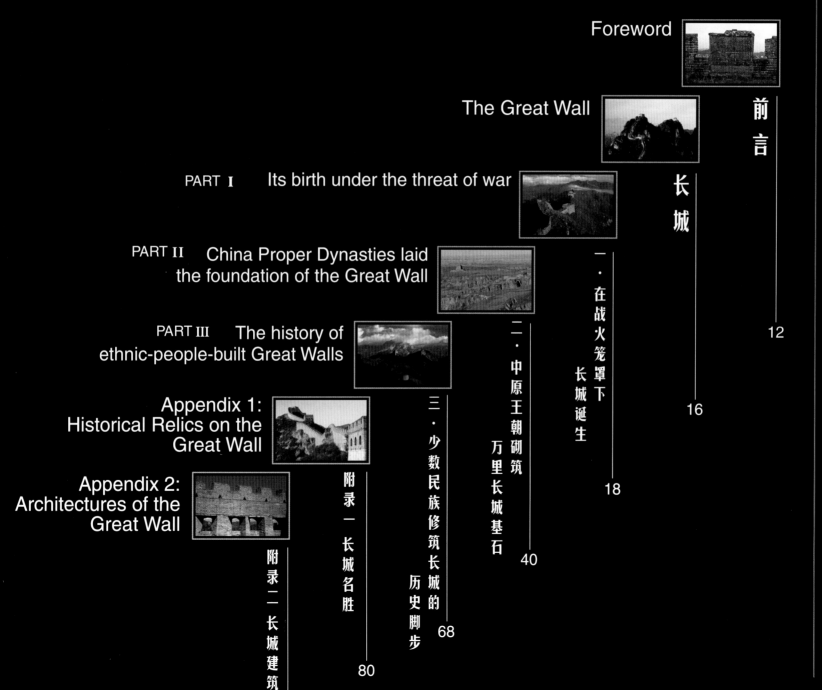

Sea clouds of Jinshan Ridge Great Wall
金山岭长城云海

Xiannu Tower Great Wall
仙女楼长城

Feeling the Sadness and Perseverance of the History

By Dong Yaohui

The Great Wall is a piece of quiet music, a masterpiece of painting, and a moving sculpture. It brings vividly the history before the eyes of modern people, helping us feel the long-faded lights and warfare of the ancient times. It truthfully records and narrates the history, telling us in the meantime the insurmountable obstacles and limitations of the previous eras. If we feel an irresistible and inseparable love for the Great Wall, then a majority of this emotion derives from the sadness and perseverance in creating the history.

The history of the Great Wall has been created by mankind. The history passes on to the stories and legends via the means of language. The Great Wall is relating the glory it has witnessed in the eventful centuries. But where were the creators of the Great Wall and the history? We touch the time-honored bricks of the Great Wall, thinking that these authors are condensed in them, for we sometimes do

see in the gray bricks and mortars the appearances of the makers of this magnificent wall.

The Great Wall is also a fruit of wisdom and aesthetic ideas exhibited in man's cultural progress. The wars in the history become worn out with the fleeting time, while the charm and glamour of the Great Wall is becoming brighter against the backdrop of the history. It does not belong to the narrow history of any dynasty or people, but is an integral constituent of the broader history of the whole mankind. Every year millions of visitors ascend the wall, immerged in beholding the fruit of the wisdom of our ancestors. The inspiration and ideas flashing in their minds transcend the confinement of nationality and ethnicity.

Like all other matters, the Great Wall also has its birth and death. This is a hard fact for us all to accept. When browsing the family albums, we calmly see the whole process of our grandma's development from a baby to a girl

Foreword

and then to a maiden; she changed into a mother at the prime age, and finally she became our grandma, with gray hair and lines-ridden complexion. We feel no agony in the process, for it is a natural course of life. Faced with the natural weathering of the Great Wall, we have to learn to appreciate the incomplete beauty, discerning a kind of happiness in a serene and melancholic air. We can invest our sentiments to enjoy the fascinating stories between the interstices and to feel the booming and vibrating spirit of the wall. The desolate remains of the Great Wall prove the coldness of the time, as well as the stubbornness of the Great Wall.

On top of the Great Wall, the history is no longer something abstract, or something beyond reach. The wall is actually the extension of the past, pouring vitality into the dying history. In climbing the Great Wall, we are tracing back the history in a sense. Viewing it on a summit, I truly realize that it is galloping nonstop among the peaks and troughs. Its running pattern resembles very much the beautiful songs from the primitive ages, captivating and lasting. Even the smallest note in it brings a force that can move the whole world and that can permeate into your blood. That is the song of the Great Wall; with this symphony, it keeps its fast paces in the long river of the human history. Feeling the Great Wall sometimes means listening to great feats, which imbibe you with the sadness of the history and which satisfy your insatiable needs and wants in reality. Sometimes, it is like feeling the life itself, for the Great Wall has swallowed innumerable lives. The message relayed by those lives is the depth and sacredness of humanity. I am a pious listener of the Great Wall and my listening will go on. Oh, the Great Wall, you have so much to tell us, both hardship and happiness for us to discriminate.

Jinshan Ridge Great Wall
金山岭长城

The Great Wall

The Great Wall is the great miracle created by various ancient Chinese laboring peoples, the spiritual symbol of their industry, wisdom, and fortitude, as well as the treasure of the world civilization. From the historical perspective, it is a product of military strategy that functioned as the permanent defensive structure in protecting the political interests of the various emperors and kings in Chinese history. However, objectively, the Great Wall has also exerted major positive influence in the history with respects to China's social-eco-nomic development, scientific and technological progress, ethnic mergence

cultural exchange, communication between the oriental and the western world, etc.

The history of building the Great Wall began very early. In the Spring and Autumn Period, the states Qi and Chu had already set up to build it. In the Warring States Period, the seven major states were independent from each other. For the purpose of defending their frontiers, the powers began to con-struct long walls along their borders, which later became the Great Wall.

In the middle and latter parts of the Warring States Period, nomadic ethnicities such as the Huns and the Tunghus, began to enter the phase of slave-holding society and the slave-owning aristocracy of these peoples fre-quently attacked the northern areas of Qin, Zhao, and Yan for the purpose of looting cattle, possessions, and slaves, therefore, the three states began to

Mutian Ravine Great Wall　慕田峪长城

set up a defensive wall along their northern borders respectively.

In 221 BC, Qin conquered the other six states and established the first totalitarian feudal empire in the Chinese history. To hold back the Huns attacks, Qin Shi Huang, the first emperor, ordered the large-scale construction of the Great Wall, which was actually an extension and connection based on the three states', namely, Qin's, Zhao's, and Yan's, original walls. Only after the reign of Qin Shi Huang did the title of the Great Wall come into being.

In the Western Han Period, the old Great Wall remained, but it was extended to the west considerably, with a total length of ten thousand kilometers, which was the longest in the Chinese history. Afterwards, dynasties such as Western Jin, Northern Wei, Eastern Wei, Northern Qi, Northern Zhou, Sui, etc. have all built some lengths of the Great Wall. Besides, Goguryeo, Liao,

Jin also built their own walls, most of which were along new routes. Today, in the northern provinces of China, there remains a nearly continuous Great Wall. It starts from the Yalu River, crossing Yan Mountain, Helan Mountain, and Qilian Mountain, snaking across the deserts and steppes, heading towards Jiayuguan Pass in the northwestern China. This imposing Great Wall was built by the Ming Dynasty, which spent most of its 277 years of ruling building this wall, representing a climax in the history of building the Great Wall.

Now, the military function of the Great Wall no longer exists, however, because of the rich historical heritage carried by it, the Great Wall has become a symbol of the Chinese spirit; it also becomes the venue for the peoples all across the globe to feel the Chinese history and to make cultural exchanges.

PART I # Its birth under the threat of war

1. The ancient pass with an eventful history

A pass in the ancient times was a stronghold guarding an important frontier place. Before the Spring and Autumn Period, the vassal states did not normally station troops at the passes. The states armies were scattered inside within their territories. When there was a war alarm, the generals would summon the troops in front of the state gate. This was recorded in many historical works, such as *Zhou Li (Rites of Zhou)*, *Guo Yu (Discourses of the State)*, etc.

Of course, there were also examples of guarding the fortresses or passes in the Spring and Autumn Period. For instances, it was recorded in *Zuo Zhuan (Commentary of Zuo)* that in the thirteenth year of Duke Wen,

Marquis Jin sent a general to station at Taolin Fortress; in the twenty-sixth year of Duke Zhao, Marquis Jin sent troops to station at Que Pass, etc. However, all these were only exceptional circumstances that had no universal significance. Therefore, Gu Donggao, a Qing Dynasty scholar, wrote an article entitled *Why The States of The Spring and Autumn Period Did Not Guard the Frontiers* in *Spring and Autumn Events List*. He cited two incidents, i.e. Duke Zhuang of Qi attacking Jin and Qin attacking Zheng, to demonstrate that it was common phenomenon in that period for states to leave their frontiers unguarded. In conclusion, he wrote, in the Spring and Autumn Period the states kept warring with each other and the world were in chaos, but at that time the frontier passes were often not strictly controlled by any troop, and that the enemy soldiers could come and go easily as in a high street.

In the later times of the Spring and Autumn Period and the beginning years of the Warring States Period, with the ever-heated fighting, standing armed forces appeared. The purpose of the war in this period has changed from looting and dominating towards annexing the enemy states. The common situation of undeveloped moats, unprepared fortresses, unfortified cities, and unexploited topography in the Spring and Autumn Period was no longer suitable for the demand of military defense. All the states began to stress fortifying the frontiers. Frontier passes have therefore become the strategic targets in the wars in order to control military routes and to counterattack the enemy. Thereafter, all states stationed troops at frontier passes. Building of city walls and moats and strengthening of frontier passes constituted a key part of the military defense strategy.

In the Warring States Period, the states employed large numbers of troops to guard their frontier passes. According to historical works,

even small states such as Han stationed as many as 100,000 soldiers to guard its frontiers. Wei also dispatched troops to protect its border areas, which consumed large sums of fund and other resources. In the *On Map of Guan Zi*, the generals were required to have a thorough understanding of the frontier situations. From these we know that in the Warring States Period, stationing troops at frontier passes was emphasized by most states, for only by strengthening defense in peaceful times could it be possible to hold back the enemy attacks in war times.

In the Periods of Spring and Autumn and Warring States, the defense of passes directly decided a state's safety as well as the outcome of war. Therefore, the various states changed their previous policy of leaving passes undefended and instead they commonly adopted measures to send troops to guard them.

2. The defense was provided by the city

The prevailing of city war strategy was an important military phenomenon in the Warring States Period. During the Spring and Autumn Period, there were not many cities and normally, although large, a city never exceeds 300 *zhang* (ancient Chinese length measure)in dimension; although large, a population never exceeds 3,000 households. For average vassal states, their capital cities have a circumference of no more than 900 *zhang*; for major ministers feudal cities, they accounted for only 1/3, 1/5, or even 1/9 of the capitals. If the number of keeps of a minister exceeded 100, it would be deemed as detrimental to his state. By The Warring States Period, the number of cities increased rapidly, so did their size. 'A city of 1,000 *zhang* or of 10,000 households was commonplace. Along with the increase in the status and function of the cities, their defense became an important component of the states defense strategy.

Strengthening cities defense was a major measure in defending a state. First, strategically, a city was the most prosperous local place where economy, politics, and culture throve. Some cities were the hub of an entire area. A city was a strategic stronghold both overall and locally, controlling the traffic routes and the economy of a whole vassal state or of a region. It became the so-called most contested place by all strategists, pivoting the whole war development. For instance, in the latter half of

the Warring States Period, the taking of Handan by the coalition forces of Zhao, Wei, and Chu in pushing back Qin's offensive towards Zhao capital, Handan; the taking of Jimo and Ju in the war between Yan and Qi. They were the critical events in deciding the victory or defeat of the wars or even in deciding the fate of the states involved. Secondly, in the offensive and defensive of a city, the enemy forces could be effectively destroyed or engaged, paving the way towards a sweeping triumph. Thirdly, cities were important supporting bases for war. The food, clothes, arms, and money were all stocked in them, thus rendering the successful defense of them a critical factor in winning a war. Furthermore, a city also provided the conscripts and could be turned into an effective troop, providing standby manpower for subsequent wars. Meanwhile, a city also served to cut off or weaken the enemy forces supply and logistics in its vicinity. In the Warring States Period, all states emphasized the construction and defense of cities; this was revealed in many an academic military work of that period. For

▽ Jiayuguan Pass
City Tower
嘉峪关城楼

example, in *Sun Zi Bing Fa (Sun Zi Art of War)* he stressed that in a war, attacking a city should be avoided as much as possible. In his opinion, It is an inferior strategy to attack a city, for in attacking a city, strength will be exhausted. Other works such as *Mo Zi, Sun Bin Bing Fa (Sun Bin's Art of War), Yu Liao Zi, Liu Tao (Six Strategies for War)*, and etc. all contribute relatively large portions in elaborating on the offensive and defensive of a city.

A city was an important defense project. According to defense requirements, a city can normally be divided into walls, moats, and gates, drawbridges, tower, watchtowers, etc. In the direction from where the enemy might come, there were several walls. The saying goes, The inner wall is called Cheng; the outer, Guo. (Both are names of walls.) In The Warring States Period, the construction of city walls mainly adopted rammed earth plus planks method. According to the exploration and pilot excavation of the Yan's Lower Capital, the construction of walls adopted the ramming earth in which sticks, ropes, or planks were added. Due to its large height and thickness, the ramming process necessitated a building process from inner to outer, or vice versa, increasing the ramming width progressively. In ramming the height, the progressive layer-by-layer method was also employed. Through the underground archaeological excavation in the past decade or so, we have accumulated a relatively comprehensive understanding of the basic scale of the Warring States city construction. For example, the excavation of Handan after

liberation found that it was divided into the King's City and Northeast Guo (meaning a wall or city). The Guo wall alone has a length of 3,200 meters from east to west; 4,800 meters from north to south; the broadest part of the southern wall reaches 20 meters. Another example, Qi's capital, Linzi had two cities: an inner one and an outer one, with the inner city's circumference being 7,000 meters and that of the outer, 14,000 meters.

As to the measures and methods of defending a city in the Warring States Period, there are plenty of clear records in various historical documents, such as *City Defense* etc. in *Mo Zi, Defense* in *Shang Jun Book, Defensive Strategy* in *Yu Liao Zi*, and etc. Roughly, the content is making complete preparation for defending a city first. Deep and wide moats, strong and thick walls, sufficient soldiers, enough food and fodder, powerful bows and arrows, and finally, sharp lances. Secondly, excellent maneuvering and disposing of troops, mobilizing and organizing militia in defending the city. Adult men forming an army; adult women, another; and the weak and the senior yet another, and dispatching the most suitable tasks to them respectively. Thirdly, building various defense projects outside the city, dismantling outside-city houses, preparing the material needed in the war, anticipating a lengthened war with more than three months stock of food and fodder. Fourthly, adopting positive defense strategy, combining tactical defense and timely surprise, and combining the methods of internally streamlining and externally seeking aid.

▽ Jiayuguan Pass
嘉峪关

3. The trace of the past

Fire was used in the alarm signaling system of the ancient Chinese military defense. When the enemy came in daytime, sending alarm by smoke or other signals; during night, by fire. It originated in the Zhou Dynasty and had been in use for more than two thousand years. It is an integral part of the ancient Chinese national defense construction.

Employing signal fire to send military alarm was very efficient and highly convenient in the ancient times when telecommunications means were lacking. The system consisted of fire towers for different directions. From the story of King You of Zhou teasing vassals by sending fire signal, we infer that at that time, a fire tower was established every certain interval between the capital to the vassal states. Straws and wood were stocked all the time such that when there came an enemy, the watchman could send off smoke in daytime and make fire in night. The next fire tower could spot this signal within no time and then relay it to the next tower along the route, alerting the frontier resident troops and vassals to counterattack and rescue in time.

In On Order of *Mo Zi*, the signal fires of the cities can be seen, smoke is raised in daytime, while fire is used during the night; *Zhou Ji (Chronicle of State Zhou)* of *Shi Ji (Historical Records)* says: King You established signal fires and smoke; in Sima Zhen's *Suo Yin (Anecdotes)* it was also made clear that smoke for the daytime and fire for the night; all these historical writings point out that in daytime, smoke would be sent off while in night, fire. These were the function of the signal fire.

In the Warring States Period the signal fire system was well established and all states built signal fire towers along their borders. The *Prince of Wei* of *Shi Ji (History Records)* says: The Prince gambled with King of Wei, then the herald reported that there was signal smoke in the north and that the enemy Zhao was invading the territory. At that time there even existed such rules that on seeing a signal fire alarm, the commander in chief could dispose troops in emergency even without his king's order. With the coming into being of the Great Wall, the signal fire system for sending alarm from afar quickly combined with it to create a better defense.

△ The Relics of Han Dynasty Great Wall of Gansu
甘肃汉长城遗址

Jiankou Great Wall
箭扣长城

4. The Great Wall, separate but connected

The Great Wall's origin can be traced to the Spring and Autumn Period in the seventh century BC, but the origin of deploying wall as a form of defense should be much older.

The archetypes of the Great Wall can be represented by the Xiajiadian Lower Layer Culture in Liaoxi Area, which has a history of 4,000 years, and are dispersed mainly in the northeast of Inner Mongolia, the west of Liaoning Province (Liaoxi Area), and the north of Hebei Province. The late celebrated archaeologist, Su Bingqi, was the first to raise in *New Probe into the Origin of Chinese Civilization* the concept of primitive Great Wall. The villages of the Xiajiadian Lower Layer Culture densely situated in a riverbed area and almost all of them had fortresses built with earth and stones, forming a complete defense structure. This is especially so alongside the River Yingjin of Chifeng, Inner Mongolia, where these tiny stone castles were connected into a line and happen to coincide or parallel with the later Yan-Zhao Great Wall. In areas such as Weichang, Pingquan in the north of Hebei Province over 70 stone castles of Xiajiadian Lower Layer Culture are discovered which form a group in line with their specific natural surroundings. The Maolangou castle group of Pingquan chose to build on the shadowy side of mountains square-shaped castles, with several smaller ones surrounding each big one. These castles have gateways, with the middle area a bit higher in elevation. Rich finds were unearthed there. These groups of small castles have two formations: one is scattering in large areas, and another is being connected alongside the borders. The latter formation served as the state's collective defense system, with a function similar to that of the later Great Wall.

That the primitive Great Wall first appeared in Liaoxi Area has a profound historical background. This area connects the China Proper and the northern China cultures, an area where agriculture and animal husbandry both flourished. It has a prosperous and systematic archaeological culture since the Neolithic Age. Differing cultural ethnicities, economic and cultural types, and cultural traditions conflicted, were interdependent with each other, and merged with each other, providing an important historical stage for the forming of a unified, multi-ethnic nation in China. The Xiajiadian Lower Layer Culture has already entered the Polity Age, and the heads of the communities used castles as an implement for them to rule internally and to defend externally.

In the Spring and Autumn Period, with the escalation of wars, the deployment of the war of maneuver and the shift towards focusing on the use of infantry and cavalry and on field war and siege war combined to render the original defense means no longer fit for the military demand. Therefore the monarchs of the various states needed to build larger-scale defense works to block the enemy from entering the inner parts of their states, while strengthening their key passes and fortresses. Thus a concept of connecting signal fire towers, castles, valleys, cliffs, moats, roads, etc. with walls came into being, with the purpose of forming a large-scale defense system along the borders. This system, unlike a castle or city that could only safeguard a single point, could protect an enormously vast area with its long defense line. Looking at it at a specific point, it is a complete defense work, having not only signal fire towers for sending alarm but also parapet for watch; not only a place for the stationed troops to live in but also a logistics warehouse. Meanwhile, on key routes, a pass that can be used to both attack and defend was built. Because of its length of miles, or even thousand of miles, and overall, it is a linear shape, hence the name, the Great Wall.

▽ The Relics of Nanzhao Chu Great Wall of Henan
河南南召楚长城遗址

5. King Cheng of State Chu ascending the frontier summit

The State Chu of the Western Zhou Period was located near Jingshan Mountain, with its capital at Danyang (now a northeast area of Zigui, Hubei). Later it moved its capital to Ying (now Jinan City to the northwest of Jiangling, Hubei). Chu was frequently at war with the Zhou Dynasty, and the Zhou people called the Chu people barbarians. Only when Zhou declined did Chu get the opportunity to grow in might along the Yangtze and the Han Rivers. In the beginning years of the Spring and Autumn Period, Chu conquered many nearby small states, but it was no match of Qi when Qi became the dominating force in the China Proper and could attack Chu at any time. Therefore Chu built along its northern borders Liecheng (rows of cities, literally) in order to protect itself from Qi invasion.

Liecheng is actually a series of defensive castles for stationing troops, an important form of defense works, which were later, transformed into the Great Wall. In the Spring and Autumn Period, Chu utilized hills, river banks and dikes, and cliffs to connect the many Liechengs into a rectangular defense system which spanned easterly from Luyangguan Pass in the southwest of Lushan Mountain, Henan, and then reversed southeastwards, and finally it reached the northeast of Biyang County. It is the earliest historical record of the Great Wall. Due to its form and structure, it was also called the square city or connected dikes by the ancient people. Therefore in the name the Chinese character that means ten thousand is not mistaken accidentally for another character meaning square, albeit the two words are almost identical except for a tiny stroke. In the Warring States Period, Chu extended these square cities westwards from Luyangguan Pass to connect Jiwang Mountain in the southeast of Luanchuan County, then turning southwards to the north of Deng County, thus completing a rectangular.

Chu's records of the Great Wall appeared first in *Zuo Zhuan (Commentary of Zuo)*. This book says that in the sixteenth year of King Cheng of Chu (656 BC), Duke Huan of Qi, together with many vassal states, attacked Chu. When the coalition forces came to Xingshan Mountain (now in the southeast of Yancheng County, Henan), Chu sent an envoy called Qu Wan to meet them. The envoy said to Duke Huan: "If you pacify the vassal states with integrity, who can resist? Chu has 'square cities' as defense and the Han River as its moat." On hearing these, the coalition forces retreated. Afterwards, many historical records can be found on how the Chu square cities held back the enemies or were bro-

ken by them. From these facts, it seems that the Chu Great Wall served critical roles in the wars to control the China Proper between Chu and other states.

The Chu Great Wall features an entire utilization of the topographic characteristics in construction. Mountains and rivers were used to build cities, with mountain cliffs as walls and rivers as moats. Along its site, many relics can be found today. Roughly, it wound from the northeast of Deng County, Henan, and passing Zhenping County it went northwards. Then it turned towards the east from the northwest of Nanzhao County, and passing the south of Lu County, it snaked towards the south from the west of Ye County. Along the sides of Fangcheng and Wuyang counties it came finally to Biyang County. But another opinion holds that it originated from the south of the Han River, Hubei.

△
The Relics of Nanzhao Chu Great Wall of Henan
河南南召楚长城遗址

▷
The Relics of Nanzhao Chu Great Wall of Henan
河南南召楚长城遗址

Jinshan Ridge Great Wall
金山岭长城

Jiankou Ridge Great Wall
箭扣长城

6. On top of the remote, strange Qi Great Wall

Qi lies in the north of today's Shandong Province, a vassal state of Zhou in the eleventh century BC. The first king was Lu Shang, with the capital Yingqiu (later called Linzi, now to the northeast of Zibo, Shandong). Lu was respected by King Wen of Zhou as the teacher and they planned for destroying Shang and reviving Zhou. In the reign of King Cheng of Zhou, Lu Shang was entitled marquis and granted a privilege to subjugate other vassal states. When Duke Huan of Qi ruled, he promoted Guan Zhong to implement reforms. After the state became powerful he began to annex neighboring states. Qi was a major state in the east, and after the many annexes of Duke Huan of Qi, it emerged as the mightiest force among the states in China.

In the seventh year of Duke Huan's reign (679 BC), shortly after Qi's hegemony, Chu became a major force along the Yangtze and the Han Rivers, showing a trend to balance Qi. Consequently, the two states made efforts in building the Great Wall even in the Spring and Autumn Period.

The earliest record of Qi Great Wall appeared in *On Weight of Guan Zi*. A sentence in the book reads: To the south of the Great Wall, it is State Lu; to the north, Qi. As to which one is the earliest, there are two competing opinions in the communities of history and the Great Wall studies. One holds that the Chu Great Wall is older; the other protests that it is the Qi Great Wall. Those with the latter opinion inferred according to the ruling time of Duke Huan of Qi and the life of Guan Zhong

that its Great Wall should be built between 685 BC and 645 BC. However, this inference is problematic. Scientifically speaking, because *Guan Zi* was not written by Guan Zi himself, but by later Taoists in the name of him. Therefore the Great Wall in the book is not sufficient evidence that in Guan Zhong's time there was already a Great Wall in Qi. In Duke Huan's rule, Qi was powerful and ambitious to dominate in the China Proper, so it is senseless for them to build such a wall that would consume their manpower and resources.

After the deaths of Duke Huan and Guan Zhong, there were riots in Qi. Chu took the chance to expand northwards. However, historical evidence is yet to be found about Qi's building of the Great Wall in this period. In the Warring States Period, Duke Kang of Qi and King Wei of Qi were recorded in the history to have built the Great Wall. The last time for Qi to build walls was in the rule of King Xuan (319 BC-301 BC). Sima Qian's *Shi Ji(Historical Records)* says: King Xuan of Qi built the Great Wall on mountains, which spanned from the ocean in the east to Jizhou magistrate in the west, totaling over a thousand *li* (Chinese length measure, equivalent to 500 meters). There are numerous records in historical documents about this part of the Great Wall and they are relatively consistent. Today some traces can still be found along its site. The Qi Great

◁ ◁ ◁
The Relics of QI Great Wall of Taian,Shangdong
山东泰安齐长城遗址

Wall started from the north of today's Pingyin, Shandong, in the west and headed towards the east to Taian County, then the north of Laiwu County, turning eastwards, via Yi Ridges and the east of Anqiu County, it ended at the seaside between Dazhu and Xiaozhu Mountains in the south of Jiao County. The Mulingguan Pass, famous for connecting the northern and southern parts of Lu since the ancient times, lies on Yi Mountain. The construction of the Qi Great Wall is divided into ramming earth one and stone one. On open fields, it used mostly ramming loess in building, while on mountains it used stones instead. The remnant parts are 1 to 4 meters in height and 4 to 5 meters in thickness.

Jinshan Ridge Great Wall
金山岭长城

7. Lonely Wei Great Wall alongside the Yellow River

Wei is a vassal state of Western Zhou, with Ji as the surname of the rulers. It was conquered by Jin (sixteenth year of Duke Xian of Jin, 661 BC) and its land was allotted to minister Bi Wan. In the first years of the Warring States Period, the descendent of Bi Wan, Marquis Wen of Wei, together with Zhao and Han states, divided Jin State. In the twenty-third year of King Weilie of Zhou (403 BC), it was recognized as a vassal state, with its capital at Anyi (now to the northwest of Xia County, Shanxi).

Since the twenty-fourth year of King Zhending of Zhou (445 BC), Marquis Wen of Wei came to power. He promoted successively Zhai Huang, Li Li, and Wei Chengzi as the Prime Minister to reform. Major achievements were made and consequently Wei became a major power in the beginning of the Warring States Period.

In the thirty-third year of Marquis Wen of Wei (413 BC), Wei began an all-out attack on Qin. It advanced as far as Zheng (now Hua County, Shaanxi). The next year Wei troops took Qin's Fanpang (now to the southeast of Hancheng, Shaanxi). In the thirty-seventh year of Marquis Wen of Wei (409 BC), Wei's general Wu Qi swept Qin's Linjin (now to the east of Dali, Shaanxi), Yuanli (now to the south of Chengcheng, Shaanxi), Luoyin (now to the west of Dali, Shaanxi), Heyang, etc.

Originally, Wei and Qin had a common border river: the Yellow River, and Wei had only one city, Shaoliang on the western side. After the taking of the aforementioned cities, all the western side area belonged to Wei. Qin had always regarded Wei's occupying the western side of the river as a major strategic failure and had been preparing the taking back of them ever since. Duke Xian of Qin also implemented a series of reforms, with successes, to strengthen the state. In the fourth year of King Hui of Wei (366 BC), Qin made an offensive on the coalition forces of Han and Wei and defeated them at Luoyang. Then, in the sixth year of King Hui of Wei (364 BC), Qin advanced to the eastern side of the River, and had a major battle at Shimen (now to the southwest of Yuncheng, Shanxi) against the Wei troops and killed sixty thousand. In the eighth year of King Hui of Wei (362 BC), Wei had large-scale wars against Han and Zhao States and Qin seized the opportunity to attack it. At Shaoliang Qin scalped the Wei forces. Qin took Fanpang city ever since and forced Wei to move its capital to Daliang (now Kaifeng). Now although Wei still had most of its west-of-river land, but already at a disadvantage. The Shaoliang Battle especially threatened the western part of Wei. To consolidate the defense of west-of-river areas, before Qin's would-begin large reform campaign, Wei sent general Long Jia to build a stretch of Great Wall along the river, i.e. the Hexi (west-of-river) Great Wall of Wei.

This Great Wall's building happened 50 years after the original Qianluo Great Wall of Qin on the same site. Its purpose was to defend against Qin and the western barbarians in the mountains. It started in the south from Huashan Mountain valley of Huayin County, Shaanxi, winding alongside the Changjian River, via Gucheng Village to the northwest of the county, crossing Wei and Binluo Rivers eastern banks, through the north of Dai County, to Dengxu Plain to the north of Dangchuan Village, then it went northeastwards into Chengcheng County, northwards to the northwest of Heyin County, then heading towards the southeast at Xichenghou Village, after passing several villages of southern Hancheng County such

as Beilongting, Malingzhuang, Chengnan, and Chengbei, it ended at the bank of the Yellow River, with a total length of over 100 kilometers. Even today, some relics remain there. This part of the Great Wall used the high banks of the Luo River, coupled with rammed earth walls; therefore it is also called Binluo Great Wall. The remnants of it can still be found in today's Huayin, Dali, Chengcheng, Hancheng, etc. of Shaanxi Province.

In 361 BC, King Hui of Wei moved the capital to Daliang (now Kaifeng, Henan) and built Great Wall in the China Proper as well. Inferring from the historical records, the walls built by Wei there started in the north from the northwest of Weijuancheng's southern bank of the Yellow River (the Warring States Period route), passing through Weijuan and Southern Ancheng from between Hanhuanyong and northern Xiuyu, then it turned southwestwards at Yuanyang County, Henan, crossing the ancient Ji River, via Zhengzhou, it ended in the mountainous land to the northeast of Mi County. Due to its origin at Juancheng on the southern bank of the Yellow River, it is also called Weijuan Great Wall or Wei's Henan Great Wall. The flooding of the Yellow River in this area has rendered the relics of this Great Wall oblivious.

8. Anecdotes of King Zhao of State Qin

The Relics of Guyuan ▷
Great Wall of Ningxia
宁夏固原秦长城遗址

▽ The Relics of Qin
Great Wall of Lintao
临洮秦长城遗址

The Yulin Area has been of strategic importance since the ancient times and the Great Wall serves as the good testimonial of this. People once said: Only when the Ming Dynasty moved Yansui Town to Yulin after the completion of the Great Wall did it become a key pass of the Great Wall. However, this opinion is not well founded. Since the Warring States Period, the Yulin Area has always been a key fortress in the north, but it throve and declined for many times, changing names in these periods, therefore adding difficulties to its recognition for later generations.

There are many sites of relics in Yulin County, and except for a few parts, they can be connected into a line. If you go on a field trip to this area you would find that to the south of the Ming Great Wall there is another remnant wall. Although the rammed earth walls are not much for clear recognition, the foundation can still be connected into a line. This remnant wall, 2.5 kilometers away from the Ming Great Wall, is exactly the relic of the Qin Great Wall in the Warring States Period.

It was said that Qin, with the surname of Ying for its rulers, was the descendents of Boyi. In Qin Zhong's times, he was entitled minister by King Xuan of Zhou. In the eighth year of Duke Xiang of Qin (770 BC), Duke Xiang of Qin was entitled vassal for his deeds in escorting the eastward movement of King Ping of Zhou. In the Spring and Autumn Period, it set up a capital at Yong (now to the southeast of Fengxiang County, Shaanxi), spreading across today's central Shaanxi and southeastern Gansu. In the rule of Duke Mu of Qin, he conquered twelve states and dominated the western barbarians. But after Duke Li of Qin, under the rule of Duke Zao, Duke Huai, Duke Jian, Duke Hui, etc., the state became weakened because of the backward economy and the frequent internal upheavals and as a result it was constantly attacked by others.

At that time, the biggest threat came from Jin in the east and Wei and Han States after the division of Jin. In the time of King Zhao of Qin, after expansion into the north, Qin was threatened by the northern nomadic peoples such as the Huns and the Linhus. Therefore, the reason for Qin to build eastern Great Wall was to defend against Jin and Wei, while the northern Great Wall against the Huns. According to historical records: in the Warring States Period, two Great Walls were built by Qin: one was built during the reigns of Duke Li and Duke Jian of Qin, when Qin built this defense structure along the western bank of the Luo River after Jin had taken its west-of-river land. The other was Qin's Northern Great Wall built after King Zhao of Qin conquered Yiqu people. The remnant Qin Great Wall in Yulin County is exactly part of the Great Wall built by King Zhao of Qin.

The Qin Great Wall on the western bank of the Luo River was built in the sixteenth year of Duke Li of Qin (461 BC). Afterwards, in the sixth year of Duke Jian of Qin (409 BC) the Great Wall was rebuilt. The purpose for Qin to build the Great Wall along the Luo River was to defend against Jin initially, and Wei subsequently.

Within fifty years, from the fact that Qin first built the Great Wall to defend against Wei and then Wei followed suit to build walls to hold back Qin we can see the trend of a thriving Qin and a declining Wei.

The Great Wall built by King Zhao of Qin was built after the conquering of Yiqu people. The Yiqu people rebelled and surrendered alternately before the rule of Duke Xiao of Qin. During King Huiwen of Qin, the power of Yiqu saw some growth and fought several battles against Qin with some successes. In the eleventh year of Gengyuan of King Huiwen of Qin (314 BC), Qin sent troops on an expedition into Yiqu territory, but due to Qin's limited strength, Qin drew back after taking a couple of cities. But Qin had always seen Yiqu in the northeast as a potential threat. In the thirty-fifth year of King Zhao of Qin (272 BC), after Dowager Empress Xuan seduced and killed the king of Yiqu at Ganquan Palace, Qin conquered Yiqu and occupied areas such as Longxi, Beidi, and Shangjun. Afterwards, Qin's borders were in direct contact with the Huns, the Linhus, etc. To forestall their moving southwards, the Great Wall of King Zhao of Qin was built. In the Warring States Period, Qin's Shangjun was located to the north of the Jiugu River near Yuhe Village, Yulin County. Even today, the remnant of this Great Wall can be seen, with large quantity of bricks and tiles from the Warring States Period, the Qin Dynasty, or the Han Dynasty.

In recent years, archaeologist workers have found many remnant parts of the Great Wall of King Zhao of Qin at places such as Lintao, Gansu, and Guyuan, Ningxia. This Great Wall was later utilized by Qin Shi Huang, the first emperor, in building the Ten-Thousand-*Li* (5,000 kilometers) Great Wall.

Mutian Ravine Great Wall
幕田峪长城

Jinshan Ridge Great Wall
金山岭长城

9. Relics of Zhao Great Wall

In the Warring States Period, the plains to the south of Yin Mountain attracted the nomadic peoples such as the Huns and the Linhus who lived to the north of the mountain with its succulent grass and abundant water resources. They began to develop southwards, making the Hetao area to the south of Yin Ridges an important place for grazing. At this time, the nomadic peoples including the Huns and the Linhus began to merge into local congregations from a former state of mutually independent tribes. A relatively large tribes federation was formed in a vast area, posing serious threats to the neighboring powers of the China Proper.

Zhao was one of the seven major powers of the Warring States Period. The founder king, Marquis Lie of Zhao, was an offspring of a Jin minister. After the division of Jin by three parties in the eleventh year of King Zhending of Western Zhou (458 BC), he was recognized by the Zhou emperor as marquis in the twenty-third year of King Weilie of Zhou (403 BC). He first established the capital at Jinyang (now to the southeast of Taiyuan, Shanxi), then moved it to Handan.

King Wuling of Zhao, named Zhao Yong, was an ambitious monarch. To terminate the threat from the north by nomads, he prepared to fight against the Huns and the Linhus. To meet the demand of this war, he first launched a dress revolution in his state.

In the China Proper in the Warring States Period, infantry was used to assist the chariots, standing on the sides with arms in hand for fighting. A large chariot could carry a dozen or so soldiers. At that time, people, be them civilians or soldiers, all wore heavy and clumsy clothing, with sleeves so long as to reach the knees, and stressed that the overcoat cover the trousers and the shoes, with a long back trailing behind the feet.

The nomadic people used individual soldiers on horse in fighting. They were agile in both riding and shooting arrows, rendering the chariots almost useless. King Wuling of Zhao made up his mind to develop cavalry, but the first obstacle facing him was the clumsy clothing worn by his men. At that time, the northern nomadic people's clothes divided the top and the trousers into separate parts, with the longer top covering no further than the knees and the trousers and the shoes were exposed outside the clothing. Suppressing successfully the conservative groups opposition, he took the lead in dressing the barbarian way in his palace and ordered all his ministers and aristocracy to change. Then he summoned horse-riding soldiers and trained the first ever cavalry in the China Proper. In the fifteenth year of King Nan of Zhou (300 BC), King Wuling of Zhao led this cavalry, coupled with chariots and infantry, into fighting and defeated in turn the Huns and the Linhus, driving them to the north of Daqing Mountain.

After occupying the southern areas of Yinshan Mountain, King Wuling of Zhao set up Yunzhong County there. To strengthen its northern frontier, he also built the northern Great Wall of Zhao to utilize the natural barrier of Yinshan Mountain.

There are few historical records about this Great Wall. Its route is believed to start from today's Xuanhua County, Hebei, then turned westwards to cross the northern Shanxi Province, winding to the northwest afterwards, it continued via Yinshan Ridges to end at a valley between Langshan and Wula mountains to the north of Wuyuan, Inner Mongolia, i.e. the ancient Gaoque.

In the past years, the archaeologist workers have found many relics of this Great Wall in Daqing, Wula, and Langshan mountains. They are of rammed earth or stones, with the biggest width being over five meters and the height no more than one meter.

Zhao's great walls in the Warring States Period, besides King Wuling's, there were two more: one was built in seventeenth year of Marquis Su of Zhao (333 BC), which is also called the southern Great Wall and can still be seen partly in Linzhang, Cixian of Hebei Province. The function of this wall was to defend against Zhao's neighbor, Wei. The Wei capital, Daliang, located only hundreds of *li* away from Handan, Zhao's capital. And the Wei city, Yecheng, which was situated on the southern bank of the Zhang River, had a mere distance of less than 100 *li*, threatening positively to Zhao. Therefore, Marquis Su of Zhao built this wall to make use of the natural barriers of the Zhang River and Fuyang River. The other was built also by this Marquis, but its starting and ending locations and the building date are badly recorded in historical records that served only to baffle the scholars. It is believed that it located roughly along the line between Feigukou Pass (Yu County, Hebei) and Yanmenguan Pass (Dai County, Shanxi).

▽ The Relics of Zhao
Great Wall of Baotou,
Inner Mongolia
内蒙古包头赵长城遗址

10. Legendary Yan Great Wall

Yan had other Chinese characters as its name with identical pronunciation. It was one of the vassal states of Zhou in the eleventh century BC. Lying in the north of today's Hebei Province and the west of today's Liaoning Province, it set up the capital at Ji (now to the southwest of Beijing) and also established a lower capital at Wuyang (now to the south of Yi County, Hebei). Yan was one of the seven major powers of the Warring States Period.

In 316 BC, King Kuai of Yan planned to reform and abdicated his throne to the Prime Minister Zi Zhi. However, contrary to his will to strengthen Yan, his act caused military coup by heir apparent Ping and general Shi. King Xuan of Qi also seized this opportunity to conquer Yan, killing King Kuai of Yan and the Prime Minister in the war. A feud existed ever since between the two states. In the twenty-seventh year of his rule (285 BC), King Zhao of Yan appointed Yue Yi as commander in chief and attacked Qi with other vassal states, taking over seventy cities from Qi. It was the heyday of Yan. However, when King Zhao of Yan died, Yan was defeated by Qi again and lost all the cities it had taken previously.

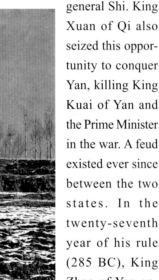

▽ The Relics of Yan Great Wall of Yi County, Heibei
河北易县燕长城遗址

According to historical records, Yan built two great walls, with one in the south and the other in the north. There were constant wars between Yan and Qi, therefore, to ward off Qi, Yan built the southern wall. Meanwhile, Qin has come to power gradually then and planned to expand eastwards, driving Zhao and threatening Yan. In this connection, the southern wall could also be used as a prop to defend against both Zhao and Qin.

About its building time, according to *Commentary on Zhang Yi* of *Shi Ji (Historical Records)*, persuade by Zhang Yi, King Zhao of Yan joined forces with Qin. On Zhang Yi's way to report this news, King Hui of Qin died before he came to Xianyang. King Hui died in the fourteenth year of Gengyuan, when it was the first year of King Zhao of Yan, or 311 BC. Therefore, it is doubtless that the southern Great Wall of Yan was built before King Zhao.

The northern Great Wall of Yan was for the purpose of warding off nomadic peoples such as Tunghu and Shanrong. This wall served as the northern barrier of Yan, which was also the last wall built in the Warring States Period. This wall lies to the north of the Ming Great Wall, starting in the west from Zhangjiakou, Xuanhua, through Weichang on the northern side of Yanshan Mountain it entered the north of Chifeng, Inner Mongolia, and Aohan County, crossing Fuxin, Liaoning, it continued to turn southwards after crossing the Liao River, via Kuandian, it then came to Liaodong, finally it ended at the northern bank of today's Chongchon River in D.P.R. Korea, with a total length of over 2,400 *li* (1,200 kilometers).

According to *Commentary on the Huns of Historical Records*, Yan had a famous general named Qin Kai, who was once a hostage of Tunghu. The Tunghus trusted him. On returning, he led a troop fighting the Tunghus and drove them 1,000 *li* back. He built a length of Great Wall from Zaoyang to Xiangping. It is said that the young hero, Qin Wuyang, who accompanied Jing Ke to attempt to assassinate Qin Shi Huang, was his grandson. Although the accurate date of Qin Kai's building the northern Yan Great Wall is not clearly stated in historical documents, but according to his relations with Qin Wuyang, the historians inferred that it was in the rule of King Zhao of Yan.

Yan has built three great walls in Inner Mongolia: one was the northern Great Wall by Qin Kai. Another was the later Chinan Great Wall. The last one was Laohushan Great Wall, which was found in 1975, lying to the south of Chinan Great Wall, with a remnant length of over five kilometers in good condition. From the excavated Yan's knife-shaped money cast with the Chinese character, Qin's Half *Liang* (Chinese ancient measure of weight, or 50 gram) Coins, and iron weights of the Qin Dynasty, we can know that this part of the Great Wall was not built by Yan alone, and the later Qin Shi Huang, the first emperor, also made use of it.

Yan had its own features in building the Great Wall. The stone Great Wall was built by laying natural rocks at both sides, then filled with pebbles and gravels, therefore making it firm. By now, it has not completed collapsed yet. The rammed earth Great Wall was constructed in even, stone-lacking areas with thick earth layers. The Great Wall normally made use of the locally available materials and was built with different methods.

Jinshan Ridge Great Wall
金山岭长城

Jiankou Great Wall
箭扣长城

The route of the Yan Great Wall spanned the area where many ethnic minorities of China actively developed this rich, vast land with hard work and industry. Tunghu was among them. It had remained a powerful nationality in the north from the Warring States Period through to Qin and Han dynasties. Its language belongs to Altaic family and was used by many peoples afterwards. Mongolian derived from Tunghu tongue, too. This people contributed much to development of the economy and culture of the northern China area.

11. Long-lost Zhongshan Great Wall

Zhongshan was a state established by the northern nomadic people, Xianyu, which belonged to Baidi branch. It located in today's Zhengding County, Hebei. With Qi to its east, Yan to the north, Jin and Zhao to the southwest, it was encircled by powerful neighbors. In the later years of the Spring and Autumn and the Warring States Periods, owing to its people's valor and wisdom, it often defeated powerful enemies such as Jin and Zhao, although it was relatively small in size. However, in 406 BC, it was once conquered by Wei troops. 25 years later, Wei was defeated repeatedly by Zhao and Qi. Zhongshan drove out Wei troops and reestablished its state in 381 BC, setting up its capital at Lingshou (now to the northeast of Pingshan, Hebei). Between 377 BC and 376 BC, this state recaptured its southern fortress, Fangzicheng, and northern pass, Zhongrencheng, which had been occupied by Zhao, and thus acquired a full independence. At that time, Wei, Han, and Zhao were busy dividing up Jin, so Zhongshan took the opportunity and developed into prosperity.

Recently, people postulate that the Zhongshan Great Wall located on the border area of today's Hebei and Shanxi Provinces and that it was built to defend against Zhao, but nothing can be said with certainty about its starting and ending positions. Zhang Weihua in *On the Building of the Great Wall of China* claims that Zhongshan Great Wall is in today's Xinle; Shou Pengfei in *The Great Wall in the Dynasties* says: this wall (Zhongshan Great Wall) begins in the north from Taixi Mountain, through Changcheng Ridge, across Hengshan Mountain, turns southwards along Taihang Mountain, and passes such as Daoma, Jingxing, Niangziguan, Guguan all belong to it. The purpose of building the Great Wall for Zhongshan was defending against Zhao, and Handan was the capital of Zhao, therefore the northward direction from the city should be where the invasion came from, and accordingly, Zhongshan Great Wall should be distributed along its southern borders. Some researches show: in 369 BC, Duke Huan of Zhongshan built a segment of Great Wall alongside the northern bank of the Huai River between its southern cities, Fangzi and Fuliu, seizing the opportunity when Han and Zhao were busy fighting Wei. The Huai River is today's Huaisha River and its branches, deriving from the Taihang Mountain in Zanhuang County, Hebei and running across today's Yuanshi, Gaoyi, Ningjin, and Xinhe counties, converging into today's Fuyang River. The route of the river changes from time to time. Fangzi locates to the southwest of the present day Gaoyi County. Fuliu lies on the eastern bank of now the Fuyang River that runs across the northwest of Ji County, Hebei.

In 314 BC, when Qi attacking Yan, Zhongshan seized the opportunity and annexed some land from Yan. Its territory now extended to the Huai River in the south, to the Yi River in the north, to Fuliu in the east, and to Taihang Mountain in the west. Now the new power, Zhao, began to plan against Zhongshan. In 300 BC, King Wuling of Zhao launched an all-out invasion into Zhongshan. By 296 BC, Zhao troops seized Lingshou and Zhongshan was terminated as a state. Later, Zhongshan was moved to Fushi (now to the south of Yulin City, Shaanxi).

In 1988, the archaeologists of Hebei Province found some remains of a stone wall on the eastern bank of the Tang River, Tang County. Afterwards, they in turn found similar sites in Quyang, Shunping, and Laiyuan. They are of two kinds: stone or stone and earth. Stone walls are mainly found at Huangtuling and Zhoujiabao and on some summits, with a wall foundation of 2 to 3 meters and a height of 0.5 to 3.2 meters varying according to topography and physical condition. Stone-and-earth walls are commonly seen at the main and branch lines of the Great Wall, which are only 1 to 2.5 meters wide and 0.4 to 3 meters high now. From the wall section of some relic walls it can be seen that the foundation is paved by large stone slates and that the two sides are laid with roughly ground stones. Gravel and earth are filled in the middle, but no rammed earth is found. The stone and earth walls are mainly found along mountain slopes and ridges, with brown earth forming the ditches. Besides, precipitous cliffs are used as walls. The typical examples are the segment between Huangtuling and Gujiabao and the segment between Shennan and Shenbei of Shunping County. The eastern bank of the Tang River is a cliff, therefore no wall was built but instead the cliffs are used as natural barriers.

Bada Ridge Great Wall
八达岭长城

PART II China Proper Dynasties laid the foundation of the Great Wall

1. Meng Tian: conqueror and the conquered

Qin General Meng Tian is recorded in Sima Qian's *Historical Records*, which says: Having unified China, Qin sent Meng Tian and three hundred thousand men to drive barbarians in the north, annex Henan, build the Great Wall, fortify the strategic points, and utilize favorable topography. He set off from Lintao and finished his expeditions at Liaodong, with a covered distance of thousands of kilometers. He crossed rivers and camped on Yin Mountain, then wound northwards. The whole feat took more than ten years to conclude.

Therefore we know that the famous General of the Qin Dynasty, Meng Tian, was in charge of building the first Great Wall. Meng Tian was a descendent of a famous general. His grandfather, Meng Ao, came to King Zhao of Qin from Qi and had achieved a lot in the wars against Han, Zhao, and Wei. He was therefore promoted to a very high rank. Meng Tian's father, Meng Wu was also one of Qin's great generals and he assisted General Wang Jian to conquer Chu. Since his childhood, Meng Tian had always been studying very hard. After he learned laws, he became an officer in charge of prison matters. In the twenty-sixth year of Qin Shi Huang, the first emperor, he was made a hereditary general. In that year, he led his troops attacking Qi and defeated the country with great success. Meng Tian was apt both in military and civil fields. He was said to be the inventor of Chinese writing brush.

In the thirty-seventh year of his rule, Qin Shi Huang died of disease at

Shaqiupintai (now to the northwest of Guangzong, Hebei) on route of his fifth inspection. Zhao Gao, in conspiracy with the Prime Minister, Li Si, established the eighteenth prince, Hu Hai, as the second emperor. At the time the first prince, Fu Su was stationed in Meng Tian's camps as a supervisor and he had an intimate personal relationship with the great general. To avoid future rebellion, Zhao Gao issued a fake imperial rescript ordering Fu Su and Meng Tian to kill themselves. Fu Su accepted the order and the sword and cut his own throat. Meng Tian was not willing to die without a proper cause. After resigning his military post, he was put into a prison at Yangzhou (now to the northwest of Zhang County, Shaanxi).

The new emperor, on hearing the death of his brother, wanted to release Meng Tian, but Zhao Gao was jealous of the great general and he concocted many crimes to defame the general. The emperor listened and sent people to kill Meng Tian at Yangzhou. As a famous general in the history, Meng Tian, together with his father and grandfather, contributed greatly in Qin's unification wars and in strengthening the frontier defense system.

At the last years of the Warring States Period and the beginning years of the Qin Dynasty, Qin put all its resources into fighting the six states; therefore it could not concentrate on defending the frontiers. Hun Chanyu, Touman, seized the chance and defeated Tunghu and Yuezhi. He then crossed Yin Mountain and the Great Wall to attack the Yellow River Hetao, Yunzhong, Jiuyuan, Shangjun, Beidi, and the counties in the western Shaanxi. Its looting posed an extreme threat to Qin capital, Xianyang, and Guanzhong area. The Huns had two hundred thousand men as main force that stationed to the west of Yin Mountain and in the northern areas of Helan Mountain.

After his successful unification of China, Qin Shi Huang began an inspection trip in the thirty-third year of his reign (214 BC), covering counties such as Jieshi, Beibian, Beiping, Yuyang, Shanggu, Dai, and Yanmen. Its route was basically along the original Great Wall of Yan and Zhao, with the purpose of collecting information about the Huns. He then made up his mind to recover the lost land and to strengthen the frontier defense. Lu Shen from Yan said to Qin Shi Huang that the people who will eventually overthrow Qin will be the Huns. This served only to further prompt the first emperor to drive the Huns. He sent Meng Tian with his 300,000 men to chase the Huns in the north and recapture Henan.

In the summer and autumn of the thirty-second year of Qin Shi Huang (215 BC), Xianyang governor, Meng Tian, with the first emperor's order, led the three hundred thousand men on an expedition against the Huns.

◁ The Relics of Zhao Great Wall, Inner Mongolia
内蒙古赵长城遗址

Meng Tian led his main force into the north of Hetao via Shangjun and Yulin; the other troops entered the south of Hetao via Beidi and Xiaoguan. The two forces drove the scattered Hun tribes along their advancements and met with no major resistance from the Huns. In the early winter, the two troops finally came to Hetao. The Huns crossed the Yellow River and fled northwestwards. The Hetao areas were then recaptured.

In the early spring of the thirty-third year of Qin Shi Huang (214 BC), Meng Tian crossed the Yellow River and took Gaoque (now to the northeast of Hangmianhou County, Inner Mongolia where Yin Mountain ends), Yang Mountain (now Lang Mountain, Inner Mongolia), and the vast land between the Yin ridges and the Yellow River. Another troop crossed the Yellow River and took Helan Mountain area. Under the great military pressure from the Qin Dynasty, the Huns fled northwards 700 *li* (350 kilometers). Then all the land lost by Qin and Zhao were recovered. The Qin Dynasty set up 34 counties in this area and assigned them to the control of Jiuyuan Prefecture.

After the wars, Qin Shi Huang ordered Meng Tian to continue his stationing at Shangjun and to build the Great Wall in order to ward off the renewed attack from the Huns. Therefore Meng Tian, on the one hand, supervised the counties to repair original Great Wall of Yan and Zhao, which wound from Liaodong to Gaoque; on the other hand, he ordered his troops to build a new Great Wall from Gaoque to Lintao. The new wall ran along Helan Mountain from the north to the south, with many high peaks and deep valleys. Therefore, this wall was not connected into a line. The mountain cliffs and valleys were used as barriers. The old and new walls formed a firm defense line against the Huns in the north with its 5,000 kilometers in length.

Another measure taken by the first emperor to consolidate his frontiers was to move emigrants. He exiled the so-called criminal soldiers and civilians to the Great Wall and forced them to guard the frontiers. To secure the supply of these troops and to strengthen Hetao and Central Government relations, Qin Shi Huang ordered Meng Tian to build a straight road from Yunyang (now to the northwest of Chunhua, Shaanxi), via Shangjun, to Jiuyuan. The straight road started building in the thirty-fifth year of Qin Shi Huang's rule (212 BC), with a total length of 400 kilometers. Its remains can still be seen today.

2. A dialogue with the Great Wall of Qin Shi Huang, the First Emperor

Although many vassal states had invested resources in building the Great Wall since the Spring and Autumn Period and the Warring States Period, the lengths were within range of hundreds of kilometers. Only the Great Wall built by Qin Shi Huang exceeded 5,000 kilometers. Therefore after his rule, the Great Wall was also called the Great Wall of Ten Thousand *Li*. (1 *li* equals 0.5 kilometers.) Even today, on mentioning the Great Wall, people think of Qin Shi Huang and he's worth it indeed.

Qin Shi Huang was born in 259 BC in Handan, the capital of Zhao, when his father was a hostage in the city.

The time when he lived was an eventful one, the critical moment for unification of China. It is said that even as a boy he had the aspiration to unify China. He liked to hear his father telling stories about Shang Yang Reform in Duke Xiao's time. Shang Yang's being executed by his political enemy made him indignant.

When he was thirteen, his father, King Zhuangxiang died and he came to the throne as the youngest king among the seven major powers. After years of war, Qin annexed Zhao, Yan, Han, and Wei. Then it attacked Chu in the south. And by 221 BC, Qin finally terminated the last power, Qi, and fulfilled its feat of unification of China.

After the unification, Qin Shi Huang established imperial system and called himself proudly the first emperor. He hoped that his descendents would continue the rule to the eternity. A nationwide administration system was also put in place, which used county as the basic unit. Local officials were assigned the task of managing local affairs. The central government had three dukes and nine ministers to assist the emperor. All officials had to be appointed or demoted by approval of the emperor.

A vast, multi-ethnic, unified China was established, which was a major contribution to the Chinese history. China's later superiority in feudal economy and in culture had an inseparable historical connection with Qin Shi Huang's unification.

After the unification, besides unified law, measure, monetary unit, writing system, etc., another move of important significance was building the famous Great Wall to defend against the Huns.

The Huns was a major ethnic people in the northern China, spreading mainly on the Mongolian plains. Their activity reached Yin Mountain in the south and Lake Baikal of today's Russia. They were a nomadic people. King Wuling of Zhao had set up Jiuyuan Prefecture in the Hetao area and today's Baotou and built Great Wall as defense. He also ordered the emigration of part of the ministers slaves to Jiuyuan to reclaim wasteland. Yan and Qin built great walls along their northern borders as well. By the end of the Warring States Period, because the states in China Proper were busy fighting Qin, the Huns occupied the Hetao areas within the Zhao and Yan Great Walls. After the unification, Qin Shi Huang sent Meng Tian in 215 BC to recapture the vast area to the south of Yin Mountain and set up 34 counties. But this campaign only drove off the Huns but did

▽ The Relics of Qin Dynasty Great Wall of Wulate, Inner Mongolia
内蒙古乌拉特秦长城遗址

Jinshan Ridge Great Wall
金山岭长城

Jinshan Ridge Great Wall
金山岭长城

not get rid of the Huns threat. To ward off the Huns from coming southwards and to safeguard the unification, Qin Shi Huang ordered the connection and repair of the original great walls of Qin, Zhao, and Yan, which consumed enormous fund, resources, and manpower. The finished Great Wall began from Lintao in the west and reached Liaodong in the east. This is the famous Great Wall of China.

Qin Shi Huang Great Wall can be roughly divided into three segments: east, middle, and west. The eastern segment begins from Huade in Inner Mongolia, via the south of Kangbao County in Hebei, the south of Taipusi and Duolun counties in Inner Mongolia, the north of Fengning and

Weichang counties in Hebei, the north of Chifeng and the south of Naiman and Kulun counties in Inner Mongolia, it ended to the north of Fuxin in Liaoning. Most of this part was based on the Yan Great Wall of the Warring States Period. It extended, according to historical records, as far as the northern bank of the Taedonggang River, Pyongyang, D.P.R.Korea.

The construction of this part used different techniques to take advantage of the topography and natural conditions. The walls at Chifeng, Weichang, and Fengning passed mountainous areas and therefore made use of the local stones. When it passed valleys, a ditch or a parallel wall was used. The water area employed stones in construction, while between two mountains natural rocks were laid as a stone gate.

There are three remains of the Great Wall in Zhangjiakou and Chengde area. The wall in the far north is also called Kangbao Sandaobian. It was built in Qin Shi Huang's rule by connecting Huade and Kangbao in Inner Mongolia and Chifeng walls, with a remaining height of 1 to 3 meters. Local people call it earth dragon. The remains in Weichang, Hebei, lies between Qianliang, Banbidian, Shanwanzi Town and Gangouliang, Laowopu Town, with a length of about 190 kilometers. The ancient Great

Wall in Chifeng, Inner Mongolia also has three sites. The Zhaowuda County archaeologist team believes, after careful inspection, that the Chibei Great Wall was built after Qin's unification. Its remains are on the ridges at Shanshuipo, with a remaining length of 30 kilometers and a height of less than one meter. Local people call it stone dragon, earth dragon, sand dragon, or cattle route. Many castles, barriers, and fire signal towers were also built alongside the wall.

The middle segment runs through the following places: Xinghe of Inner Mongolia, the northern bank of Huangqihai, the northern Jining, Daqing Mountain, Chayouzhong County, Nanwubulang in the south of Wuchuan County, Damiao, Yinhao, and Xidoupu of northern Guyang County, Yin Mountain, the Yellow River, Wuyuan, northern Hangjinhou County, Wulanbu, and the northern verge of the desert. This part was built on the basis of Zhao Great Wall after Meng Tian drove the Huns northwards. The part between Yin Mountain and Helan Mountain should have been built after Qin's unification.

This part mainly used stones because of its location on Daqing Mountain and Yin Mountain. Many repair traces can be seen in the stone walls found in the south of Wulatezhong County. Alongside the wall, both within and without, many fire signal towers are found. The passageway in the valley has some castle-like structures for defense. Alongside the Yellow River many castles can be seen as well, called barriers in history.

The western segment was built utilizing the Yellow River as natural barrier, focusing passes and castles instead of a connected line. Between

◁ ▽
The Relics of Qin Dynasty Great Wall of Wulate, Inner Mongolia
内蒙古乌拉特秦长城遗址

Jiankou Great Wall
箭扣长城

Helan Mountain and Yin Mountain, the Great Wall should have been merged by the sand dunes because of the moving deserts, if built at all. There are still traces of Qin Shi Huang's Great Wall in Guyang County.

The Kangtugou Great Wall used the mountainous topography and the local materials. On mountains, rocks were used, while on plains, loess was rammed into walls. Its fire signal towers selected the high but smooth ridges inside the Great Wall.

Although many contributions were made to the Chinese history, Qin Shi Huang was a feudal emperor and the general representative of the exploiting classes. After annexing the six states, he invested large sums of resources into building mausoleum and palaces. He sent people to look for panacea for him, too. Fighting the Huns and building the Great Wall finally consumed up the country's resources. According to statistics, the population at that time was twenty million, but military and labor services accounted for 2.2 million of them, 11 per cent of the total population, with most of which young adults. This extreme exploitation and suppression rapidly exasperated the tension between the land owning class and the peasants. In the second year after the first emperor's death, the first peasant rebellion burst out finally, burying the Qin Dynasty as a result.

3. The Han Great Wall advancement and exploration

An important incident in the history is Mayi Stratagem, indicating a drastic change of policy by Emperor Wu of Han, Liu Che, from one of peace and amity to one of large-scale wars. The name of the incident was acquired because it took place at Mayi City. The history of building Great Wall in large scale by the Han Dynasty also started from this period. Mayi City located between Pianguan City and Ningwuguan Pass, to the north of today's Shuo County, Shanxi.

Liu Che was a key figure in the history that, after Qin Shi Huang, consolidated the feudal system. After coming into power, the biggest challenge facing him was the threat from the Huns in the north. In June of the second year of Yuanguang (133 BC), a minister, Wang Hui, suggested a surprise ambush of the Huns for the purpose of recapturing the vast area to the south of Yin Mountain and of expanding into west-of-river areas. Emperor Wu of Han convened with his cabinet, meeting many's opposition. But he finally opted for a strategic change from defense to offense and designed the Mayi Stratagem to seduce the enemy.

Although the effort was abortive, the large-scale wars against the Huns by Emperor Wu of Han began. From the Mayi Stratagem in the second year of Yuanguang to the flee of the Huns in the fourth year of Yuanshou (119 BC), Emperor Wu of Han chose Wei Qing and Huo Qubing as Commander in Chief to launch three large-scale, decisive military campaigns.

According to historical records, Emperor Wu of Han's building of the Great Wall also commenced in this period. Emperor Wu built the Great Wall in four times: the first was in the second year of Yuanshuo (127

BC), when General Wei Qing attacked Loulan from Longxi. Large-scale repair of the Qin Shi Huang Great Wall began. The second time was in the second year of Yuanshou (121 BC); General Huo Qubing led several dozens of thousands of cavalry troops to meet King Hunye and King Xieudu of the Huns on the Qilian Mountain slopes. After the victory, the west-of-river area was under the control of the Han Dynasty. To secure the safety of the Hexi Corridor, Emperor Wu ordered the building of the Great Wall spanning from today's Yongdeng to Jiuquan, Gansu. The third time was from the sixth year of Yuanding (111 BC) to the first year of Yuanfeng (110 BC), from Jiuquan to Yumenguan Pass. The fourth time was from the first year of Taichu (104 BC) to the fourth year of Taichu (101 BC), from Yumen to Lake Lop Nur.

From the second year of Yuanshou (121 BC) to the fourth year of Taichu (101 BC) of Emperor Wu of Han, a route know as the Silk Road was created, connecting the China Proper to the west, and alongside the road,

△ The Relics of Han Dynasty Great Wall of Gansu
甘肃汉长城遗址

a firm, imposing Great Wall was finished to guard the traffic on it.

Although more than ten dynasties in the Chinese history have taken part in the building of the Great Wall, only Qin Shi Huang, Han, and Ming Great Walls exceeded five thousand kilometers in length. Han Great Wall is the longest of the three, spreading from Liaodong in the east to Xinjiang in the west with a length of ten thousand kilometers.

Large number of remains can be found in today's Yin Mountain areas, Inner Mongolia, and the Hexi areas, Gansu.

The eastern segment of the Han Great Wall leaves relics from the eastern Shangdu, Inner Mongolia, to Liaodong Peninsula. The Han Great Wall in Chende area, Hebei, lies to the south of the Yan and Qin Great Wall and to the north of the Ming Great Wall. From Dayingzi, Ningcheng County, Inner Mongolia, the wall enters Cheziliang, Huanzigou, Sandaogoumen Town, and Chende County, Hebei. It then goes southwestwards to Shuangmiaoliang, Zhiyun Town. The height is about 1.5

△ The Relics of Yangguan Pass Great Wall
甘肃阳关长城遗址

meters, with a width of 8 to 10 meters and a remaining length of about 15 kilometers. Every two kilometers a terrace-shaped structure was built, without any connecting wall between two such structures. This kind of structures continues westwards to Liugouying, Bugugou Town, then a wall of 3.5 kilometers in length reappears between Erdaoying and Sandaoying, Xiaoluanhechuan, western Longhua. After that, again, only terrace-shaped structures remain until Miyun County. There are no less than 100 such structures altogether, mostly built at the converging area of two streams or important mountain valleys. They are square, with the upper part being smaller than the lower part. The sides are 8 to 12 meters in length, with a remaining height of 1.5 to 3 meters. Local people call

them gun emplacements or steamed breads.

Segments of the Western Han Great Wall can also be found near the Xiyang River, Huaian County, Zhangjiakou, Western Hebei. Many terrace-shaped structures and Han tombs are found as well within the vicinity. Local people call such structures earth castle. The Han Great Wall in Hebei Province also emphasizes the utilization of natural barriers, with a combination of terrace-shaped structures and walls. The walls were built with rammed earth, mostly. Horse face structures also appear on the Han Great Wall near Huaian. Besides, a fire signal tower was built every half-kilometer.

The Han Great Wall in Chifeng, Zhaowuda County, Inner Mongolia, lies to the south of Qin Shi Huang Great Wall and the Yan Great Wall of the Warring States Period. Dozens of terrace-shaped structures, castles, or cities are found nearby too.

The Han Great Wall remains in Liaoning Province winds eastwards from Fuxin, Liaoning, via Zhangwu, Faku, Kaiyuan, then turns southwards, via Xinbin and Kuandian, enters into D.P.R. Korea.

The middle part of the Han Great Wall lies between the west of Shangdu and Ejina County, Inner Mongolia. The outer wall built during the rule of Emperor Wu of Han adopted a double-line form, spreading on the deserts and plains to the north of the Qin Great Wall. The construction of this part adopted a combination of rammed earth and stone laying, or used cliffs as walls. Many cities, castles, passes, and fire signal towers were also built alongside this wall. These military facilities were generally built inside the wall. The frontier cities were smaller than inland cities, with office buildings, warehouses, barracks, and civilian buildings in them. The city walls were generally built by ramming earth, and the gates were built with extrawalls. Some frontier cities adopted inner and outer walls. Passes were used as the headquarters of military troops guarding the frontiers, normally located near the wall, similar to a military watchtower. It is smaller than a frontier city, with walls and a singular gate. Barbican entrance was built, with the corners of the wall protruding outwards, forming the later horse faces. The fire signal tower was used as an alarm system, mostly built on summits or plains, alongside the wall, with an interval distance of 0.5 to 1 kilometer. Those built on summit used stones and was shaped like a pyramid, with some of them built with circular walls. Those built on plain mostly used rammed loess, with a width of the foundation between 7 to 8 meters and a height of 3 to 4 meters. Sometimes circular walls were built, too.

The western part of the Han Great Wall starts from Lake Sugunur, Ejina County, Inner Mongolia, then it winds down the Ejina River, turns

Simatai Great Wall
司马台长城

Yumenguan Pass, Gansu
甘肃玉门关

westwards at the Beida River, Jinta County, Gansu, via the southern side of Bei Mountain and the Sule River, it comes to Xiaofangpan City (where located the Yumenguan Pass stationary troops in the Han Dynasty) that lies to the northwest of Dunhuang County. It then extends towards the Kongque River via Lake Lop Nur without building walls, but only continuous fire signal towers.

The walls and fire signal towers in the Han Dynasty in Juyan region were for the purpose of cutting off the connection between the Huns and the Qiangs, relying on the only traffic route to the West Hexi Corridor. The remaining sites, over thirty in number, include walls, fire signal towers, military offices, and official offices. The western part of the Great Wall was basically built with rammed earth or adobe, with reed between the earth layers to strengthen the wall against weathering. Parts of it were built using coarse stone slabs as frames filling with pebbles or pebbles with boughs.

Yumenguan Pass and Yangguan Pass were both important gateways to the West in Han dynasty and the most critical passes in the Han Great Wall. They were the hub points on the Silk Road connecting the southern and the northern roads, exerting extremely important influence on the communications, cultural, and economic exchanges between China and the rest of the world.

It is said that the quality jade as tributary goods from Hetian and other places of the West had to be brought into China through Yumenguan Pass via Tarim Basin, hence its name (in Chinese, Yumenguan means the pass or gate for jade).

The Han Yumenguan was set up in the third year of Yuanfeng (108 BC) of Emperor Wu of Han. After its establishment, it had witnessed three prosperities and three declinations within 200 years. Since Wei, Jin, and South and North dynasties, due to the frequent wars, the Silk Road became desolate, and so did the Yumenguan Pass as a result. By the Tang Dynasty, a new northern road, i.e. through Anxi and Hami, was used to go to the West. Therefore, the location of the Han Yumenguan Pass, the famous ancient pass, became a riddle in people's memory.

In the last century, Chinese and foreign archaeologists came to the deserts to solve this old riddle. Between 1907 and 1915, a Hungarian with British nationality called Stein had conducted two excavations in the Han Great Wall remains in Dunhuang. He got 789 pieces of Han bamboo slips with writing on them. One of them that he collected from an ancient mail stop remains, which located 90 meters to the northwest of Xiaofangpan City, had readable characters, saying Yumen Military Officer, therefore he claimed that he has found the remains of the ancient Yumenguan Pass for the Han Dynasty to control its traffic to the West. In 1944, Xia Nai and Yan Wenru from the former Northwest Scientific Investigation Group History Team conducted testing excavation near Xiaofangpan and its northern side of the Han Great Wall and fire signal towers and found 38 pieces of writing bamboo slips, with one of them reading, Jiuquan Yumenguan Pass Military Officer or the like. The history community has since regarded Xiaofangpan as the site of the ancient Yumenguan Pass.

Xiaofangpan lies about 90 kilometers to the northwest of Dunhuang County. The city is square in shape, with relatively complete walls that are built with rammed earth. The east-west length is 24.5 meters, and the south-north length 26.4 meters, with a remaining height of over 9 meters. In the southeastern corner of the city lies a horse road that is less than one meter in width and runs alongside the eastern wall until the top of the wall. The Han Great Wall turns westwards after passing this city, connecting directly with Yangguan Pass. There is also a segment of Great Wall 2.5 kilometers to the northwest of this city, heading for Lake Lop Nur.

An archaeologist, Mr. Chen Mengjia, postulated in 1965 that the site of the ancient Yumenguan Pass was not Xiaofangpan, but to the west or northwest of it. He believed that even given the aforementioned Han bamboo slips as evidence Xiaofangpan could only be described as the military office site of the Yumenguan Pass, but not the pass itself.

In 1979, the archaeologist team from Gansu Museum and Dunhuang

The Relics of Han Dynasty Great Wall of Gansu
甘肃汉长城遗址

County Cultural Institute conducted a scientific excavation at the Maquanwan Fire Signal Tower 11 kilometers to the west of Xiaofangpan after completing their investigation of 71 similar fire signal towers located in Dunhuang County. They found 1,217 Han bamboo slips, on which many clues were discovered regarding the site of Yumenguan Pass, the highest official of the Pass and his duties, the activities of the stationed troops, etc. On one of the wooden tablet was written: Yumen Eternal Fire Signal. The scientific workers therefore concluded, taking into account of the new discoveries and the investigations, that Chen was right and that the site should be near western Maquanwan.

So far no completely acceptable conclusion is reached as to where is the site of Yumenguan Pass. Further evidence in archaeology is to be added to solve this hazy riddle.

Now, Xiaofangpan and its nearby sites are listed as Gansu provincial cultural relics protection unit. In 1983, special grant was allotted to repair the eastern wall of the city and to make an iron gate. Special personnel were sent to guard it.

According to historical records, Yangguan located to the south of Yumenguan Pass. South is yang, while north yin, therefore the name of Yangguan.

Yangguan has been the object for many poets in the history. When Monk Xuan Zang brought Buddhist scriptures from India, he passed Yangguan. Cen Can, a poet, also wrote: in the second year I was assigned a post and twice I passed Yangguan. However, since the Tang Dynasty, this celebrated Yangguan became obsolete in historical records. Like Yumenguan, its site becomes a riddle. Why did it lose trace in the history? Now historians have found an answer: the deterioration of the natural conditions. The wars and large scale land developing have ruined the vegetation and water sources there, and accordingly, the wind and sand from the southwest gradually moved to the northeast. The Yangguan Oasis reduced in size and people were forced to move eastwards. Around the Song Dynasty, when all people move out, Yangguan was finally swallowed by shifting sands.

But where is it?

In 1972, when a cultural relics census was conducted, archaeologist workers found a city remains that was 10,000 square meters in size in the desolate desert after crossing 14 sand ridges to the west of Gudongtan. In excavation, rows of houses were found, together with rammed earth walls. Han Wuzhu coins, bronze arrowheads, Han gray pottery shards, arable land patches, kilns, water canals, etc. were also discovered. These workers made initial judgement based on their finds that this was the site of

the ancient Yangguan. In 1979, the Han Great Wall Team made up of experts from Gansu Museum and Dunhuang County Cultural Institute found for the first time the wall connecting Yangguan with Yumenguan.

There is a distance of over 70 kilometers between Yangguan and Yumenguan, with walls connecting them. Even today, the remains of this part of the Great Wall can still be found occasionally, with a height of about ten to dozens of centimeters and dozens of fire signal towers remains. The several signal towers located to the south and north of Gudongtan are in relatively good condition. The signal tower on top of Dundun Mountain to the north of Gudongtan has a remaining height of about five meters, built with earth adobe and reed. These remains show that the newly discovered site is doubtlessly the site of the ancient Yangguan, therefore solving the thousand-year-long riddle.

Yangguan Remains is now the Gansu provincial cultural relics protection unit. Recently, special grants have been allotted by Gansu Province to built iron fence and houses for the protection of it.

▽ The Relics of Yangguan, Gansu
甘肃阳关遗址

4. The long history of Sui Great Wall

In the Yulin Area, Shaanbei, there are not only Qin and Ming Great Walls, but also Sui Great Wall. Three of the four Great Walls built by Han nationality rulers, i.e. the Qin, Han, Sui, and Ming Great Walls, pass the Yulin Area, proving the great military importance of this region in the history.

In the first year of Dading (581) of the Emperor Jing of Northern Zhou, Yang Jian usurped the emperor and established the Sui Dynasty. In the third year of Kaihuang (583) of Emperor Wen of Sui, Daxing (now Xi'an, Shaanxi) was made the capital. In the ninth year, Chen was conquered and China was united after over 200 years division since Eastern Jin.

After establishment of the new dynasty, Emperor Wen of Sui implemented a series of policies that were beneficial for the unification and consolidation of the country as well as for the recovery and development of the social economy. As a result, the national power grew rapidly and the country was peaceful. The purpose for the Sui Dynasty to build the Great Wall was to defend against the northern Turks. The Turks lived in today's northern Junggar Basin and the upstream of the Yenisey River as early as the fifth century. In the first year of Yuanqin of Western Wei (552), the Turks conquered Rouran under the support of Western Wei and established a local Turk state centering on the Orkhon River, called Turk Khan by the historians. At the beginning of the Sui Dynasty, the Turks were in their heyday. To check the continuous attack from the Turks, Sui built the Great Wall to strengthen the defense.

In May of the second year of Kaihuang of the Sui Dynasty (582), Shabolue Khan, together with other khans, led four hundred thousand troops to break the Great Wall and advanced southwards. Gao Baoning attacked Pingzhou (now Lulong, Hebei). Emperor Wen of Sui decided to counterattack the Turks. Sui won the war in the end and greatly weakened the Turk khans as well as intensified the internal conflictions among them. The Sui Dynasty seized the opportunity and in turn subjugated khans such as Shabolue, Abo, Datou, etc. Peace was restored along the northern borders and Sui eliminated its distraction on the way of conquering Chen.

According to historical records, Emperor Wen of Sui built the Great Wall in four times:

The first was in April of the first year of Kaihuang (581). Jihu was sent to build the Great Wall, which took twenty days to finish. The segment of the Great Wall built by this time should be in the northern Shanxi Province. The second time was in the fifth year of Kaihuang (585). 30,000 men were sent to Suofang and Lingwu to build the Great Wall, which started in the west from the eastern bank of the Yellow River in today's Lingwu, Gansu, via Jingbian, Hengshan, Yulin, etc., Shaanxi, it finally ended at Suide. The third time was in the sixth year of Kaihuang. One hundred and ten thousand men were dispatched to build the Great Wall. The fourth was in the seventh year of Kaihuang. About ten thousand men were sent to accomplish the task. The job of the last two times was mainly to repair and strengthen the existing Great Wall, besides some castles.

In the fourth year of Renshou of Emperor Wen of Sui (604), Emperor Wen was killed by heir apparent Yang Guang, who usurped as Emperor Yang of Sui. After his coming to power, Emperor Yang moved the capital to Luoyang. More than two million men were dispatched every month to build the new capital. After its completion, another one hundred thousand men were sent to dig a long canal of over one thousand kilometers. This canal started from today's the Yellow River at Longmen, Hejin County, Shanxi, via Gaoping of Shanxi, Ji County and Xinxiang of Henan, and crossing the Yellow River, it passed Kaifeng and Xiangcheng to end at Shang County, Shaanxi.

During the rule of Emperor Yang of Sui, besides the digging of this great canal, two large-scale building and repairing of the Great Wall were also conducted. The first time was in July of the third year of Daye of Sui (607), nearly one million laborers were sent to build the Great Wall, which started from Yulin in the west and ended at the Ji River (today's Hun River) and took ten days to finish. The second time was in March of the fourth year of Daye of Sui (608), a quarter of million men were assigned to build the Great Wall, which started from Yulin Valley and wound eastwards. These efforts were not invested for strategic reasons, but for Emperor Yang's showing off his military might.

△ The Relics of Sui Dynasty Great Wall of Ningxia
宁夏隋长城遗址

Jiankou Great Wall
箭扣长城

5. Early Ming Great Wall covered in dust

The Ming Great Wall is the most time-consuming, as well as the largest in scale of engineering, the most complete defensive project in terms of system and structure in the Chinese history. It drew on previous building experience and exhibited great accomplishment in architecture and great wisdom of the ancient people.

After the collapse of the Mongolian Empire, the remnant of the Yuan Dynasty retreated to the north of the desert, continuing their reign relying on the aristocracies of the Mongolian tribes. Some of the aristocracy members could not accept the Empire's fall and dreamt to stage a comeback and to rule the China Proper again. The son of Emperor Shun of Yuan, Ayu Sridara, was the representative of this mindset, who led the remnant Yuan troops to Helin in the north of the desert (today's Harhelin, Mongolia) with the same Yuan as their state sobriquet. He often sent a large number of cavalry troops to loot and attack along the Great Wall.

In the fifth year of Hongwu of Ming (1372), the first Emperor of the Ming Dynasty, Zhu Yuanzhang, appointed Xu Da as the expedition commander in chief and Li Wenzhong and Feng Sheng as commanders, each of who was allotted fifty thousand soldiers, to drive away the Yuan remnant troops from three directions.

The famous general, Xu Da, was an accomplished military officer who

▽ The city wall of Jiayuguan Pass 嘉峪关城墙

△ The Relics of Yumenguan Pass 玉门关遗址

looked down upon the Yuan remnant troops. He was too eager to win the battle and therefore he overlooked some factors in his military maneuvers. He did not take into account the fact that infantry was mixed with cavalry in his forces and that large troops was not suitable for mobile fighting and therefore he ordered his men to chase the enemy too far to be sensible. When his troops reached Lingbei area, they suddenly met the ambush by two Mongolian forces led by Koko Temur and He Zongzhe. The Ming troops were defeated with a casualty of thousands of men. Xu Da had to retreat to the Great Wall to assume a defensive position.

In the meantime the left vice commander, Li Wenzhong, led the eastern troops to enter Yingchang, Saibei (now the western bank of Dalahaizi, Inner Mongolia), via Juyongguan Pass. Later he came to the Luqu River (now the Kerulen River) area and made it his base. A general called Han Zheng was sent to guard the fodder and food and he himself led the selected cavalry with twenty days foodstuff in advancing as quickly as possible. When they came to areas near the Tushu River, the Aluhun River, etc., they fought several times against small numbers of Mongolian cavalry troops with some victory and defeat. Then he advanced to Chenghai, today's southeastern Kebuduo, and the Mongolians were fled away. The eastern troops finally returned fruitless.

The right vice commander, Feng Sheng, and his western troops arrived at Xiliang (now Wuwei, Gansu) in May. They chased the Mongolians to Yongchang and much enemy material was seized. After leaving some troops to guard it, he ordered his men to advance toward Jiayuguan Pass. When they came to Yijuannai, i.e. today's southwestern Anxi, the Yuan general Buyantiemur surrendered. It was in June, the hottest of the year. The desert heat was unbearable, but the western troops forgot day and night in their pursuit of their enemy. They advanced as far as Shazhou (western Dunhuang County) and returned with great victory and honor.

The outcome of the three troops expedition into Mobei was unexpected by the court. The commander in chief's middle troops lost several dozen thousands of men and retreated to the Great Wall for defense. The left vice commander's eastern troops achieved nothing after much effort. Only the right vice commander, Feng Sheng's western troops won victory after victory, recovering many important passes and cities on the northwestern borders.

After this expedition, the first Ming Emperor, Zhu Yuanzhang realized that the remnant Yuan power was hard to eliminate in the near future and he accordingly changed his strategy to focus on defense. Military offices were established at various important borders cities and castles and large numbers of troops were sent to guard them. A defensive strategy relying on the Great Wall was formed.

The early Ming Great Wall projects were mainly building smoke towers, castles, moats, etc. on the Northern Wei, Northern Qi, and Sui Great Walls. In some segments, earthen walls were replaced by stone ones. Zhu Yuanzhang ordered Xu Da to build Juyongguan and Shanhaiguan Passes, Feng Sheng built Jiayuguan Pass and 12 watch towers 10 kilometers away from the Shanhaiguan. In Yongle time, much effort was invested in building fire signal towers and building stone walls and digging deep moats. In Xuande times, some castles were built. The Ming troops relied on these towers, castles, and moats as supporting base against the remnant Yuan troops.

▽ The Juyongguan
Pass Great Wall
居庸关长城

Jinshan Ridge Great Wall
金山岭长城

6. Mid-Ming Great Wall on the burnt ground

Although the Ming Dynasty began to build the Great Wall defense line as soon as the dynasty was established, but if a statistical table was made about the building times, manpower and fund invested, and the number of stationed troops along the Great Wall, we can find that among all the Ming emperors it was in the Zhengtong Period of Emperor Ying of Ming that large scale, comprehensive building occurred, especially after the Tumubao Incident in the fourteenth year of Zhengtong.

The Tumubao Incident is an incident that almost rendered the Ming Dynasty collapsed by Emperor Ying of Ming's capture by Mongolian Wala tribe. Because the incident was happened at Tumubao (Earth and Wood Castle) hence the name of the incident. The place lies now on the northern bank of Guanting Reservoir, southeast of Huailai County, Hebei Province.

Oirat was a branch of Mongolian people that became powerful in the Zhengtong Period of the Ming Dynasty. In the fourth year of Zhengtong (1439), the Oirat leader, Esen, came to throne and began to march westwards to expand. By the twelfth year of Zhengtong Period, he united all Mongolian tribes and acquired a vast land covering Liaodong in the east and Xinjiang in the west. The ambitious leader, Esen, on seeing the corrupt Ming court, believed that his time to march southwards had finally come. In the fourteenth year of Zhengtong (1499), on an excuse that the Ming Dynasty had insulted his attribute missionary, sent four troops to launch large-scale military campaigns against Liaodong, Xuanfu, Datong, and Gansu. The fire signals on Ming's northern borders were set on continuously. Under the advice of his favored eunuch, Wang Zhen, Emperor Ying ignored all other sensible suggestions and ordered his defense department to summon half a million troops within two days and to head for Datong hastily on 16th of July.

On the tenth of August, the army reached Xuanfu, when Oirat troops broke the Great Wall defense line and came for fight. Key generals such as Wu Kezhong, Zhu Yong, Xue Yuan, etc. died in war in turn. On the thirteenth, Emperor Ying retreated to Tumubao, where four sides were mountains and highly unfavorable for stationing troops. The arbitrary Wang Zhen ordered the troops stay for camping. At night, Oirat troops traced the Ming troops to the campsite. On dawn of the fourteenth, Oirat troops encircled Tumubao and cut off all water sources. The Ming troops were in dire straits. On the next day, Esen feigned retreat and sent people to negotiate for peace. Emperor Ying was desperate to get out of the situation and sent his men to negotiate too. When Wang Zhen moved his campsites near the water sources, Esen ordered attack. The Ming troops were besieged by Oirat cavalry troops. Due to mistaken command, the Ming troops collapsed. Fifty officers including key minister Zhang Fu and military minister Kuang Ye were killed and over one hundred thousand men were lost. Emperor Ying was captured.

After this incident, Oirat and Tartars continuously looted the borders, forcing the Ming Dynasty to build its northern Great Wall and castles. Consequently, a defensive network with Datong, Xuanfu, Dushi, and Maying as the first line, Juyong, Baiyang, Yanmen, Zijing, etc. as the second, and Capital Zhuozhou, Baoding, Zhengding, Yizhou, etc. as the third. Now the Great Wall that is familiar to us and that winds from Jiayuguan Pass in the west to Hushan, Dandong, in the east. To effectively manage the defense and building of the Great Wall, nine defensive regions were made, i.e. Shanhai, Ji, Xuanfu, Datong, Shanxi, Yansui, Ningxia, Guyuan, Gansu, and Mingjiu. Each region was under the leadership of a single military officer, with subordinate officers for different defensive points.

▽ Mutian Ravine Great Wall
慕田峪长城

7. Late Ming Great Wall idyllic scenery

In the later years of the Ming Dynasty, the Great Wall areas were in peace with Mongolia. This was derived from Longqing Peace Negotiating. This referred to the historical incident, which ended the military antagonism between the Ming Dynasty and Mongolian Altan tribe. Because the peace making process happened in Longqing Period of Emperor Mu of Ming, hence it acquired its name.

In the forty-fifth year of Jiajing (1566) and the first year of Longqing (1567), Gao Gong and Zhang Juzheng entered the Cabinet in turn and became the Prime Minister respectively in the third year of Longqing (1569) and the sixth year of Longqing (1572). They changed Yan Song's strategy and streamlined internal administration. Externally, they focused on strengthening the Great Wall defense project and transferred famous anti-Japanese generals such as Tan Lun and Qi Jiguang to head important cities such as Jizhou. In the meantime they also suggested peace making with Altan tribe.

In the winter of the fourth year of Longqing (1570), the artful solution of Altan's grandson, Bahannaji's, running to the Ming Dynasty for asylum finally facilitated the peace making process between the two enemies, ending the decades-long war along the Great Wall. In March of the fifth year of Longqing (1571), Emperor Longqing issued edict and made Altan King Shunyi. His followers were also given official posts accordingly. Furthermore, many markets alongside the Great Wall were permitted to trade with Mongolian tribes.

The horse markets at that time were divided into two categories, official and non-official ones, allowing the Mongolian tribes to trade the Chinese agricultural and craft products with their farming products. The official markets were used for the Mongolian tribes to trade with the Chinese government.

In the period of Longqing Peace Negotiating, Khan Altan was aging, but with assistance from his third wife, he could still exert effective control over the tribes. In the ninth year of Wanli (1581), Altan died at the age of 75. His third wife came into power and had administered for the next twenty years. She strengthened the political, economic, and cultural connections between the Mongolians and the Chinese. After the pacification of the northern borders, the Ming Dynasty's major threat from the Jurchens in the northeast became prominent and the Ming Dynasty therefore shifted its defense efforts eastwards. In the beginning years of Wanli, the military commander at Liaodong, Li Chenliang, expanded the border areas and established six towns including Kuandian and Gushan. He later repaired the frontier walls, which wound from Mianzhou to the Sancha River in the east, then from the river to the old Liaoyang. The project focused on hollow watchtowers, with bricks and stones as wall. Xiong Tingbi continued his efforts in repairing the walls and castles. After the loss of Liaodong, the Ming Dynasty shifted all efforts in managing Shanhaiguan Pass, making it a firm defense line featuring a combination of walls, castles, and fire signal towers, providing protection to the capital city.

▽ Gubeikou Great Wall
古北口长城

Bada Ridge Great Wall
八达岭长城

Jinshan Ridge Great Wall
金山岭长城

8. Qi Jiguang's thought lost on the Great Wall

In the twenty-third year of Jiajing (1544), Qi Jiguang took over his father's post to be a military officer at Dengzhou, in charge of the military households there. In the twenty-seventh year of Jiajing (1548), he was ordered to lead his men to guard Jizhen. From then on, within five

years, he regularly went to guard a place near the Great Wall every year. Then the northern borders were in tension with the Altan tribes, which frequented the Great Wall vicinities in Hebei, Shanxi, and Shaanxi. In the twenty-ninth year of Jiajing (1550), the famous Gengxu Incident occurred in the Ming history. Anda tribes encircled the capital, when Qi Jiguang was taking a military examination and he took part in the defense of the city.

In the thirty-second year of Jiajing (1553), Qi was promoted and assigned the task of defending against the Japanese pirates on Shandong seashore. From that time onwards, he shifted from defending against the northern nomadic enemies to warding off the Japanese along the coastal areas, until in the first year of Longqing (1567) he was transferred once more to guard the Great Wall. Now he had become a famous general with his many feats in fighting the Japanese on the sea.

When he came to the capital, he was in charge of the military training of Jizhen, Changping, Liaodong, and Baoding. Then he doubled as the military commander of places such as Jizhou, Yongping, Shanhai, etc. He located two major issues about the Great Wall defense line: the first was lack of manpower. The army soldiers then were lazy and proud; the new conscripts were mainly local civilians without proper military training; the soldiers transferred from other places were too tired to fight. The second problem was that the Jizhen Great Wall was too near the capital city. When war came, the court ministers tended to interfere with the military matters, rendering the generals confused and undecided.

Two fields became his concentration. First, he stressed training. The veteran general deeply understood that without a powerful military force, nothing could be achieved. He summoned three thousand Qi troops from Zhejiang, which had been established when fighting the Japanese. After

a period of training, great improvement was achieved. To summarize his experience in training soldiers at Jizhen, he wrote a valuable work called *Records of Military Training*.

Secondly, he emphasized repairing and consolidating the Great Wall and building hollow watchtowers. The Jizhen Great Wall, although it had been repaired in the years of Jiajing, had many defects. The wall was thin. The stone structure on top of the wall could neither provide shelter to soldiers, nor could it store arms. Therefore Qi proposed the construction of a new watchtower, which is the hollow watchtower that can still be seen today and that was built with bricks.

Since the spring of the third year of Longqing (1569), Qi began to arrange the hard project of consolidating the walls and building hollow watchtowers. By the fifth year of Longqing (1571), the whole project was accomplished. From that time on, the Great Wall has become even more imposing on top of the hills and mountains, with the new watchtowers adding glamour to it. After the completion of the new watchtowers,

◁ Jinshan Ridge Great Wall
金山岭长城

◁ The relics of city tower
城台遗迹

◁ City wall and fort barbette
城墙及炮台

Shanhaiguan Pass
山海关

Qi Jiguang allotted 30-50 soldiers for each of them, with storage of necessary arms and fodder. Each watchtower was led by an officer in charge of fighting. Two more officers were assigned to take charge of arms and logistics.

In the meantime of repairing the wall and building the watchtowers, he never for a moment neglected his training of the troops. First of all, he established chariot companies, with new, cutting edge weaponry. Incompetent officers were removed. A new tactic featuring the coordination of chariot, cavalry, and infantry was implemented.

In defending the Great Wall, Qi was firmly opposed to the former conservative strategy. In his opinion, to be successful in defending must be backed by an ability to fight. Defending should be based upon fighting. Therefore, he stressed the in-depth defense of the Great Wall. When the enemy came and broke the Great Wall defense, what lied in front of them would not be a defenseless plain but a well-prepared battlefield. Different roles were assigned to encircle, ambush, counterattack, or otherwise fighting the enemy. In countering the enemy forces, the infantry would be attacking in turn under the cover of the chariot and firearms. Then the cavalry would advance into the enemy. Now the Great Wall became a barrier for the enemy to retreat.

During the ten years when he was in office, due to his positive training of the troops and his efforts in repairing the wall, coupled with the Longqing Peace Negotiating with Altan in the fourth year of Longqing (1570), the Great Wall areas were basically in peace. Qi was honored many times for his military accomplishments and was promoted to very high rank.

9. Qing troops attacking the Great Pass

In the seventeenth year of Chongzhen of Ming (1644), the rebellious peasants led by Li Zicheng established a state in Xi'an called Dashun. Later, he led his troops to cross the Yellow River in the east and attacked into Beijing. Emperor Chongzhen, who changed fifty Prime Ministers in his 17 years reign, hanged himself on Mei Mountain in dismay. Li Zicheng occupied Beijing.

At that time, only Shanhaiguan Pass was not in his control. Then Li Zicheng coerced Wu Sangui's father, Wu Xiang, when in custody in Beijing, to write to persuade his son to surrender. High post and handsome money were offered in return. After careful weighing, Wu Sangui decided to surrender to the rebellious peasants. On his way to Beijing he met his folks who fled Beijing at Yongping (now Lulong County, Hebei). They told him that his father was mistreated in Beijing and that his favorite concubine, Chen Yuanyuan, was taken by a general of Li Zicheng. On hearing this news, Wu became furious. He led his men to drill at Shanhaiguan and swore to fight the rebellious forces and to revenge for the late emperor, Chongzhen. Learning that Wu changed his ideas, Li led 100,000 troops to attack the Pass on 13 April 1644. Wu knew relying on a single city he could in no way resist the attacking troops. He then sent envoy to Dorgan, the regent of Qing, which had been ambitious about taking the China Proper, and expressed his will to surrender to Qing.

Dorgan was more than happy because Shanhaiguan Pass was extremely critical on his way to taking Beijing, with the title of the No.1 Pass in the World. He had suffered a series of defeats previously. Now Wu was willing to surrender, he immediately ordered his men to enter the Pass.

On 21 April, Dorgan came to the place 7.5 kilometers away from the Pass. On 22 April, Li Zicheng engaged Wu Sangui at Shihe to the west of the Pass. Wu Sangui knelt down in welcoming Dorgan on Huanxiling Mountain, asking them to join forces in fighting Li Zicheng. However, the Qing troops did not participate at once. When the rebellious peasants and Wu had been fighting for half a day and both suffered great losses, the weather became very stormy. Dorgan believed that now was the time to join and ordered Ajige and Dodo to attack from the right wing with 20,000 men. The rebellious peasants were defeated quickly because they had been too tired to resist the new forces. Li fled the scene with some soldiers and the rest of his men were annihilated by the Qing troops.

In the beginning of May, Dorgan led his army into Beijing. In September of the same year, Emperor Shunzhi entered inside Shanhaiguan Pass. A rule of Qing, which lasted over two hundred years, began.

▽ Shanhaiguan Pass
City Tower
山海关城楼

Jinshan Ridge Great Wall
金山岭长城

PART III The history of ethnic-people-built Great Walls

1. Hopeless Northern Wei Great Wall

In reviewing the history of the Great Wall we find that nearly half of it was built during the rule of ethnic peoples. Since Qin Shi Huang, Han nationality dynasties such as Han, Sui, and Ming all had invested greatly in building the wall. Dynasties ruled by ethnic peoples such as Northern Wei, Northern Qi, Northern Zhou, Liao, and Jin also took part in building it. Therefore, we can say that the Great Wall is created by various Chinese peoples in the history.

The Northern Wei was the one that invested the most among the aforementioned five ethnic peoples in building the Great Wall. In the fourth century, the Tuoba tribe of Xianbei people occupied today's northern Shanxi and most of the Inner Mongolia. They established a country called Dai. In the twelfth year of Jianyuan of Former Qin (376), Dai was conquered by Former Qin. By the eighth year of Taiyuan of Eastern Jin (383), Former Qin was defeated by Eastern Jin and the northern area was divided. Now the Tuoba Xianbei regained some vitality and became powerful. In the eleventh year of Taiyuan of Eastern Jin (386), the Tuoba Gui selected Pingcheng (now Datong, Shanxi) as capital and became Emperor. He changed the name of the country to Wei, called Northern Wei by historians. After its establishment, Northern Wei annexed in turn Later Yan, Xia, Northern Yan, and Northern Liang and united the northern area in the fifth year of Taiyan of Emperor Taiwu (439). Now it faced Song in the south.

Since the later years of the fourth century and the beginning years of the fifth century, Rouran people throve on the Mongolian grassland and developed into a power that could resist Northern Wei in the north. Under the circumstance of antagonism with Song in the south, Northern Wei naturally regarded Rouran's prosperity as threat. In the rule of Emperor Daowu of Northern Wei, Rouran was attacked and thousands of horses and cattle were taken as prize. Rouran leader, Shelun, led his forces to retreat to Mobei to prepare future revenge. By the fifth year of Tianxing of Northern Wei (402), when Shelun had become Khan, Rouran had controlled the Liaodong peninsula. It now had a territory covering Yanqi, Xinjiang, and the northern and southern areas of the desert.

The major enemy of Northern Wei was Song; therefore they could not invest too much effort in dealing with Rouran. Emperor Mingyuan of Northern Wei decided to follow the strategy of Qin and Han dynasties in defending against the Huns and build at its northern borders walls to ward off Rouran, for the purpose of avoiding two-line fighting in realizing its ambition of southward expansion.

According to the history, the first time for Northern Wei to build Great Wall was in the eighth year of Taichang (423). This wall wound from today's Chicheng, Hebei, in the east to Wuyuan County in the Inner Mongolia in the west. This wall contained Rouran's southward movement from military perspective and cut off the connection between Rouran-controlled area and the China Proper from economic perspective. Therefore, Rouran people continued to attack this wall but without much gain due to the ascending power of Northern Wei.

In April of the second year of Shenjia of Northen Wei (429), Northern Wei launched an attack on Rouran. Northern Wei was then under threat from both the north and the south. If it attacked Rouran in the north, Song in the south did not dare to attack Northern Wei. But if Rouran's military challenges were left unchecked, the south would seize the opportunity to attack and thus putting Northern Wei in dire straits.

After this campaign, to protect the capital and to contain the northern nomadic Rouran's military attacks, six important military stations were built to the north of Pingcheng, called six towns in the history. They were, from west to east, Woye (now to the southeast of Wulateqian County, Inner Mongolia), Huaishuo (now to the southwest of Guyang, Inner Mongolia), Wuchuan (now to the west of Wuchuan, Inner Mongolia), Fuming (now to the southeast of Siziwang County, Inner Mongolia), Rouxuan (now to the west of Shangyi, Hebei), and Huaihuang (now to the northeast of Zhangbei, Hebei). Large numbers of main force troops were stationed in these military towns.

The sites of these towns and the castles and moats attached to them,

such as Baidaocheng (now to the northwest of Hohhot, Inner Mongolia), have been largely found. For example, the ancient city, Suducanggenchang, is the site for Woye Town; the ancient city, Bailingnao Kulun, is the site for Huaishuo Town; the Wulanbulang Earth City is the site for Wuchuan Town; the ancient city, Baiyinchagan, is the site for Rouxuan Town; Wulanhua Earth City is the site for Fuming Town; etc. these towns are all built with rammed earth, with horse faces, watchtowers, and gate towers. The foundation size of the walls is larger than that of the Han dynasties. Some are built with gate facing the south, others with two gates in the south and the north, with a few with three gates. Core military works are built inside the towns on high foundations. Outer cities are sometimes built to the north of the towns, or on the southern banks of rivers, with the rivers as natural barriers. Outer guarding works are sometimes built to support the defense of the towns. The defense direction of the six towns is the north. Take Bailingnao Kulun, i.e. Huaishuo Town, as an example. It lies 15 kilometers away in the southwest of Bailingnao, Guyang. This point connects Guyang in the south and Guangmo in the north. Its topology of a basin controls the important passageway to the south side of Qing Mountain, exhibiting very important military significance in defending against the northern enemies. These military towns were built for the sole purpose of military defense. Although the Northern Wei authorities tried to build uniform cities and towns, but as military defense works, the actual site and form of town had to take into account factors such as the enemy, topography, and fighting requirements.

△ The Relics of Shengjinguan Pass of Zhongwei, Ningxia
宁夏中卫胜金关遗址

Another time for Northern Wei to build in large scale the Great Wall was in the seventh year of Taipingzhenjun of Northern Wei (446). According to the history, at the time over 100,000 men from four magistrates, i.e. Si, You, Ding, and Ji, were dispatched to build the wall that wound from Shanggu to Yuhe in the west, a span of 500 kilometers. This was actually a Great Wall protecting Northern Wei capital, Pingcheng (now Datong, Shanxi).

Later, when Northern Qi built the Great Wall, it made use of partly the Northern Wei Great Wall. When the Ming Dynasty was building Datong Town Great Wall, it also basically followed the old Northern Wei Great Wall direction.

The spring of Great Wall
春到长城

2. Clouds recording silently the miracle on grassland

In the eighth year of Wuding of Eastern Wei (550), the son of Gao Huan, Gao Yang, was the Prime Minister and Lord of Qi in Eastern Wei. He used his power to usurp as Emperor Wenxuan of Northern Qi by dethroning Emperor Xiaojing of Eastern Wei. His country was called Qi, designated as Northern Qi by historians, with the capital at Ye (now Linzhang, Hebei), covering an area now to the east of Luoyang, including Shanxi, Hebei, Shandong, Henan, and part of the Inner Mongolia.

Northern Qi had a history of twenty-eight years and six emperors. Although it has a short history, it focused on building the Great Wall very much. It northern Great Wall was mainly used to defend against the Huns and the Khitans, while its western Great Wall was used to check the eastwards advancement of the Northern Zhou and Western Wei.

The northern Great Wall was built mostly by Emperor Wenxuan, i.e. Gaoyang. There were five times of large-scale construction of the Great Wall between the third year of Tianbao (552) and the eighth year of Tianbao (557).

Huangluling is now located in the northwest of Fenyang, Shanxi Province. Shepingshu is now Wuzhai County, Shanxi Province. This part of the Great Wall, with a length of two hundred kilometers from south to north, was built in the first time for the northern Qi regime.

In the middle of the sixth century, the Huns became powerful, which was active on the Mongolian grasslands. It drove off Rouran and established a Hun dynasty and in the meanwhile planned to attack the northern borders of Northern Qi. In the sixth year of Tianbao (555), one point eight million men were sent to build the Great Wall, with a total length of 450 kilometers from Beixiakou, Youzhou (now to the north of Changping, Beijing), to Hengzhou (now Datong, Shanxi). Xiakou, Youzhou, in Northern Qi is today's Nankou, Juyongguan Pass, in Changping District, Beijing. The Yu River (today's upstream of the Wenyu River) ran southwards from the Pass, so called Xiakou, meaning lower mouth in Chinese. Hengzhou was originally old Northern Wei capital, Pingcheng (now Datong, Shanxi), governing an area as far as the eastern bank of the Yellow River in the west. From it geographic position, we conclude that this northern Qi Great Wall have been built by repairing the northern loop of the part of the Great Wall from Shanggu to the Yu River built in the seventh year of Taipingzhenjun of Northern Wei (446).

In the seventh year of Tianbao (556), the Great Wall was built from Zongqinshu, Xihe (now Fenyang, Shanxi) to Yuhai in the east, with a total length of over 1,500 kilometers. Every five kilometers a station was built. And every strategically important point was built with a township, and twenty-five such townships were finished in total. This part of the Great Wall should have been built by connecting the Huangluling Shepingshu Great Wall built in the third year of Tianbao (552) and the Xiakou Hengzhou Great Wall built in the sixth year of Tianbao. The Great Wall between northeastern Xiakou and Yuhai in Youzhou did not make use of the old Great Wall foundations of the Warring States Period, Qin, and Han dynasties at the junction of Hebei and Inner Mongolia, but instead it was built alongside the southern slope of Yanshan Mountains towards Bohai Sea at today's Qinhuangdao, Hebei.

To strengthen defense, the Northern Qi also built several segments of the Great Wall inside its northern border Great Wall, called then double walls. In the eighth year of Tianbao, another double walls was built inside the Great Wall, from Kuluoba (now to the southwest of Shuozhou County, Shanxi) to Yuwuheshu (now to the northeast of Pingxingguan

◁ The Relics of Qi Great Wall of Zhangjiakou
张家口齐长城遗址

Pass in Fanshi County, Shanxi), with a length of over 200 kilometers. From an analysis of the topography and situation of that time, this Great Wall should be built in the northeast of Pianguan, Shanxi Province, along Guancen Mountains southeastwards, via Shenchi and Ningwu, it turned northeastwards. Then it ran along the Hengshan Mountains, via Dai and Fanshi Counties it ended at Lingqiu County. The Ming-built Shanxi Great Wall was basically along this direction.

After the large-scale Great Wall construction in the years of Tianbao of Emperor Wenxuan, in the years of Heqing of Emperor Wucheng, Taihangshan Great Wall was built and in the years of Tiantong of Emperor Houzhu, the Great Wall between eastern Datong to Yuhai was built.

The scales of the construction in Heqing and Tiantong Periods were very small. The Great Wall project in the first year of Tiantong was only consolidation and repair of the Great Wall between eastern Xihe and Yuhai

built in the seventh year of Tianbao of Emperor Wenxuan.

After years of building and repairing, the Northern Qi Great Wall finally formed tow major lines. One was alongside the outer northern borders, extending northeastwards from today's Luya Mountain and Guancen Mountain in northwestern Shanxi Province, via Datong, Yanggao, and northern Tianzhen, it came into Zhangjiakou and Chicheng County, Hebei Province. Then it wound alongside Yanshan Mountains southeastwards to end at sea in Qinhuangdao, Hebei. The other was inner double walls, from Pianguan in the northwestern Shaanxi southeastwards. At Ningwu County it turned northeastwards, running alongside the Hengshan Mountains, it entered Hebei Province. Then it wound northwards along Taihang Mountain, connecting the outer Great Wall at northwestern Beijing. The Northern Great Wall laid foundation for the later Ming Great Wall in selecting route.

▽ The Bada Ridge
Great Wall
八达岭长城

3. The choice of the brave

Liao was established in the beginning of the tenth century by Khitan leader Yelu Abaoji. In 916, Khitan was used as the title of the new country. In 947, it changed its name to Liao. In its heyday, its territory covered an area spanning today's Japan Sea in the northeast, outer Xing'anling and Sea of Okhotsk in the north, the middle of Mongolia in the northwest, Tianshan Mountain in the west, and bordering Song in the south along today's Meihe of Tianjin, Bai County of Hebei, and Yanmenguan Pass of Shanxi. In 1125, Liao was conquered by the Jurchens, ending its 210-year rule of the northern China by its nine emperors. The northern China area ruled by Liao was a multi-ethnic region. Besides, there were also

Sheng Jurchens, Shiwei, Zubu, Tieli, Wure, Wugu, Dilie, etc. These tribes were generally rebellious under Liao's rule, especially Wugu and Dilie. In addition to its many military quenches, Liao Dynasty built a Great Wall along the western side of Hulunbuir Grassland. This Great Wall spanned today's China, Russia and Mongolia, with a total length of about 700 kilometers, built

△ Simatai Great Wall
司马台长城

◁ Yinchuan Druma-tower
银川鼓楼

during the times of Emperor Shengzong, Yelu Longxu, and Emperor Xingzong, Yelu Zongzhen.

Wugu and Dilie tribes originally lived near the Halaha River, the Wursun River, and the Lake Hulun, basically nomadic peoples. After Khitan's prosperity, to vie for the control of this ideal farming land, these

Imperial tombs of ▷
Western Xia regime
of Yinchuan
银川西夏王陵

peoples frequently came into war against each other. After conquering Wugu and Dilie, Liao divided them into many smaller tribes and migrated them to remote areas. Those migrated to Sanhe (in Chinese meaning three rivers, referring to the three branches of the Erguna River: Gen, Derbur, and Haur) are called Sanhe Wugu. The Wugu and Dilie who

▽ Fire Signal Tower
长城烽火台

were moved to the Wululiugui River (a branch of the Erguna), Outer Baikal, included Wuwei Wugu, Dielu Dilie, Babu Dilie, Beidi Dilie, etc.

According to *Biography of Emperor Taizu* in *The History of Liao*, there were Wugu tribes too in northeastern Liao (today's northeastern Jilin Province) and Abaoji dispatched special official to govern in their territory. The Wugu and Dilie tribes in the north continuously rebelled because of the severe suppression of the Liao government. To contain them and to defend against tribes such as Zubu, Liao built this part of the Great Wall and stationed troops there.

This Great Wall started from an ancient city 2 or 3 kilometers to the southwest of Shangkuli, Erguna County, Hulunbuir City, Inner Mongolia, in the east. Then it entered Labudalin (the site of today's county government) from the southwest. The total length of this part was 20 kilometers. From Labudalin, it wound westwards on the grasslands alongside the southern bank of the River Gen, via Geluohuoyidi Mountain, Xiaogu Mountain, and Heishantou Town, it reached Sika. From this position, it turned southwards to Erdenituoluohuikalun after winding alongside the River Erguna for 35 kilometers. Then it ran northwards, crossed Erguna, and entered the former USSR after 23 kilometers. This part was about 100 kilometers, with only tiny remains that are difficult to discern sometimes. The point where this part of the Great Wall entered the

△ Yuhuang Pavilion of Yinchuan 银川玉皇阁

former USSR is between Gapuchagur and Bogedanuofuka sentry posts. It had a length of 120 kilometers in the former USSR. Then it returned into China after running 15 kilometers southwest of Outer Baikal.

The Great Wall entered Manzhouli, China, 3 kilometers west of the 60th boundary mark, Tabentuoluohaiebo. From this marker it turned southwestwards and entered Xinbarhuyou County, Inner Mongolia. Via the south of Chaganlegai Mountain and the north of Hailahennaixilei Swamps it came to the China-Mongolia 635th boundary mark from where the Great Wall exited China again. This part of the Great Wall had a length of 60 kilometers.

4. Grassland whirlwind
that no longer blows

On the Inner Mongolia prairie and north of the Qin and Han Great Wall, there lies a Great Wall that is rarely known to people, which is the Jin Great Wall. It is the one among over ten Great Walls in China that locates in the very north and that is the longest wall built by Chinese minority regimes.

Its building method is different from other Great Walls in the history. In any dynasty, building Great Wall all have used moats for walls locally. However, the proportion of this moat is always small. Jin Great Wall, in sharp contrast, adopts almost entirely this method in building. The excavated earth was used to build the wall. At some critical points castles were built and troops were stationed. Between castles, fire signal towers or ditches were used to connect them. Therefore, the defensive work built by the Jin Dynasty is called border ditch or frontier castles.

Jin was a regime established by the Jurchens in northern China. The origin of the Jurchens could be traced to very primitive eras. It was called Sushen at first, then in Southern and Northern Dynasties, it was called Wuji and in Sui and Tang dynasties, Mohe. In Five Dynasties, the Jurchens were active along the downstream of the Songhuajiang River and the Heilongjiang (Amur) River, engaging in fishing and hunting. By the fourth year of Tianzan of Emperor Taizu of Liao (925), Liao conquered Bohai. At the time, Jurchen as a name of people appeared. In the fourth year of Zhenghe of Northern Song (1114), the leader of the Wanyan tribe of the Jurchens, Aguda, rebelled the Liao regime. In the next year, he formally established a country called Jin and made himself Emperor, with the capital at Duhui City (now to the south of Acheng, Heilongjiang). In the third year of Tianhui of Emperor Taizong of Jin (1125), Jin conquered Liao and in the following year, Northern Song was also conquered. Its territory covered Japan Sea, Sea of Okhotsk, and Outer Xing'anling in the northeast, today's Mongolia Republic in the northwest, and bordered on Western Xia at Hetao, Hengshan Mountain of Shaanxi, and eastern Gansu.

In the later years of the twelfth century and the beginning years of the thirteenth century, the Mongolians, under their prominent leader, Genghis Khan, throve on both sides of the great desert, Damo. In the sixth year of Taihe reigh under Emperor Zhangzong of Jin (1206), Genghis Khan established a Mongolian country. To ward off the Mongolians, Jin began to build the Great Wall.

Mutian Ravine Great Wall
慕田峪长城

The early historical records about the Jin Great Wall are about the Taizhou Ditch made by Poluhuo. Taizhou located to the southeast of today's Baicheng, Jilin. According to historical records, Poluhuo took office in Taizhou during the rule of Emperor Xizong of Jin (1135-1148); therefore, this part of the Great Wall should have been built during this period.

During the years of Dading of Emperor Shizong of Jin, although many suggestions were made about repairing frontier castles and digging ditches, actually very small efforts were made. In the third year of Dading (1163), vice Prime Minister Wanyan Shoudao was in charge of the north. He moved the old castles near inner land along the northwestern and southwestern roads to frontier areas and connected them with Taizhou's frontier castles. The defensive works finished during the years of Dading were of very inferior quality, and consequently, within very short time, their defense worth was lost entirely.

When it came to the years of Mingchang of Emperor Zhangzong of Jin, the power of the Mongolians became even stronger, while that of the Jin regime was in decline. Therefore, the Jin government had to adopt a totally passive defense strategy against the Mongolians. The Prime Minister Wanyan Xiang first raised the issue of building the Great Wall. Emperor Zhangzong approved. After the completion of his project between Linhuang and Beijing, other local governments followed suit in digging ditches and building walls. In the third year of Cheng'an of Emperor Zhangzong of Jin (1198), the northwestern governor, Dujisizhong, alone mobilized three quarters of a million men to build the Great Wall. But the Jin Great Wall failed in the end to defend against the Mongolians and the Jin history of nine emperors and 120 years was terminated.

Over the centuries, the people on the Inner Mongolian prairie have been calling the Jin Great Wall Genghis Khan Great Wall, but this only expressed their admiration and reverence toward the great leader.

Bada Ridge Great Wall

八达岭长城

Xiannu Tower Great Wall
仙女楼长城

Kylin Screen at Jinshan Ridge Great Wall

金山岭长城麒麟影壁

Jinshan Ridge Great Wall
金山岭长城

Jinshan Ridge Great Wall
金山岭长城

Jiankou Great Wall
箭扣长城

Appendix 1 :

Historical Relics on the Great Wall

Hushan Great Wall （虎山长城）

The Hushan Great Wall locates near the bank of the Yalu River in Liaoning Province, 7.5 kilometers to the northeast of Dandong. It is the beginning of the Ming Great Wall in the east.

In the past, when people talked about the Great Wall they referred to Shanhaiguan as the beginning in the east, not knowing Hushan, Dandong. As to the reason, first, when in the twenty-second year of Hongwu (1389) Xu Da planned to build the Great Wall, he chose Shanhaiguan as the beginning in the east, while the Liaodong Great Wall was built in the beginning years of Zhengtong. Secondly, after the Manchurians entered the Shanhaiguan Pass, in their wars against the Ming troops and in their repairing of the

frontier defensive works, the original simple Liaodong Great Wall was mostly dismantled, while the Shanhaiguan Great Wall was left untouched. Finally, the imposing Shanhaiguan Pass and Jiayuguan Pass lie respectively in the east and the west, strengthening people's impression that Shanhaiguan is the eastern beginning of the Great Wall.

To protect these important remains of the eastern beginning of the Great Wall and to tap on the natural resorts in Dandong area, the Dandong government has repaired for

two times the Hushan Great Wall. In 1992, 3.8 million yuan (RMB) was invested to repair 600 meters, recovering initially the eastern beginning of the Great Wall. In 2002, 22.3 million yuan (RMB) was put into repairing the main body of the Great Wall that has a length of over 1,000 meters and into paving a road for visitors and tourists.

Xingcheng Ancient City （兴城古城）

The Xingcheng Ancient City is the only Ming city in good conditions in China. It locates in the middle of the Liaoxi Passageway in Liaoning Province, facing Bohai Sea and connecting Shanhaiguan in the west and Jinzhou in the east. Its position is of great military importance, rendering it the most sought after place for military commanders as well as a famous cultural hub with rich historical heritage.

To strengthen the defense against the Jurchens, in the third year of Xuande of Ming (1428), this city was finished and called Ningyuan. In the next year an outer city was completed. Towers were built on top of the four gates, and watchtowers were also built for the four corners. Between the inner and outer walls a moat was designed. Ningyuan's

military value became more and more obvious. The Ming troops and the Later Jin Troops engaged for many times in war at this location. The most famous of the wars was the one in which the Ming general, Yuan Chonghuan, defeated Nurhaci's troops, called Ningyuan Victory in the history.

Jiumenkou （九门口）

It lies at the junction of Suizhong County, Huludao, Liaoning, and Funing County, Qinhuangdao, Hebei. Its ancient name was One Piece of Stone Pass, famous as the No.1 pass east of capital and as an important pass along the Ming Great Wall.

In the thirteenth year of Hongwu of Ming (1380), the Ming government sent Xu Da to lead his men and local civilians to repair and build 32 passes including Yongping. Jiumenkou was built at this time. In the first year of Jingtai of Ming (1450), local official, Zou Laixue repaired and built the various cities between Xifengkou and One Piece Stone Pass and Jiumenkou became an important gateway for entrance and exit of the pass.

The Jiumenkou Great Wall used nine water gates to connect into drawbridges, with a length of 116 meters, a height of 10 meters, and a width of 23 meters. Each water gate was of 5 meters in width, equipped with double-layer double-piece two-way giant wooden doors. During the dry seasons the doors were closed to defend against the enemy, while during the flood periods, they were open to let out the water and not to affect the flow of the river, forming a miracle of city on water, water in city.

The No.1 Pass in the World – Shanhaiguan Pass （天下第一关——山海关）

Shanhaiguan is the famous No.1 Pass in the world, locating 15 kilometers northeast of Qinhuangdao, Hebei. It controls the gateway from North China to Northeast China. In the ancient times, people praised it as the unmatchable key point between two capitals and the number one pass on the Great Wall.

Its name originated from Ming's Shanhaiwei. Today's Shanhaiguan was built in the fourteenth year of Hongwu (1381), square in shape, with a moat that had a circumference of about 8 *li*, a width of 5 *zhang*, and a depth of about 2 *zhang* (*Li* and *zhang* are ancient Chinese measure units). The walls were laid with bricks as exteriors, with rammed

loess and mortar between the brick exteriors. The wall had a height of about 14 meters. There were four gates: the eastern one was called Zhendongmen. A tower was built on top of each gate, with only the eastern gate tower remaining, i.e. the tower of the No. 1 pass in the world. The gate tower is 13.7 meters in height, and the base is 11.75 meters in height. The top of the tower is 24.45 meters high from ground. If you come from the east, then you can see the imposing tower from tens of miles away. The western eave of the tower is hanged with a giant board with white as background, reading The No. 1 Pass in the World. The board was written by Xiao Xian, one of the 32 calligraphers of the Ming Dynasty in the eighth year of Chenghua (1472). Outside the four gates, special wall structures called Wengcheng and Luocheng were designed. Due to its critical geographic position, in the history, many a war occurred at Shanhaiguan.

In 1961, Shanhaiguan was listed by the State Council as a National Key Cultural Relics Protection Unit. After many repairs sponsored by the state government, it now has become a tourist resort of nationwide fame.

Temple of Mengjiang （孟姜女庙）

This temple is also called Chaste Woman Temple, locating on Fenghuang Mountain, Wangfushi Village, Shanhaiguan District, and Qinhuangdao City. According to legend, it was built before the Song Dynasty. It faces the south on the mountain. Its front gate has a flight of 108 stone steps as an access. In the front hall there is a clay statue of Mengjiang in plain clothing and wearing a sad expression. The rear hall originally had been devoted to Guanyin, a goddess in Buddhism. There is giant rocks in the backyard, with the left hand side rock carved with three Chinese characters, Wang Fu Shi, meaning Waiting for husband to return. On the right hand sight rock a poem authored by

which are said to be the footprints of Mengjiang left on her thousand-kilometer search for her husband. Behind the rocks there are Zhenyi Pavilion, dressing table, washing basin, etc.

The Temple of Mengjiang was built according to one of the four major folktales of China, i.e. Liang Shanbo and Zhu Yingtai, White Serpent, Niulang and Zhinu, and Mengjiang. According to the folktale, Mengjiang's continuous cry made hundreds of kilometers length of the Great Wall fell

Laolongtou （老龙头）

From the eastern gate of Shanhaiguan, the Great Wall extends southwards for 4 kilometers and enters the sea waves. The part of the Great Wall that enters the sea is called

Laolongtou, meaning the head of an old dragon. The segment of Laolongtou that was built using stone slabs was built in the seventh year of Wanli of Ming (1579) by Jizhen military commander, Qi Jiguang, and his general, Wu Weizhong. In the meantime a Minghai City with a circumference of 0.5 kilometers was also built. Later, defense minister, Wang Zhizhong, built a Chenghai Tower near the southern wall of Ninghai, which had a height of about 10 meters. A horizontal tablet was inset in the wall, with many poems by Qing emperors and celebrities. Chenghai Tower has been visited for many times by Qing emperors. From Emperor Kangxi to Emperor Qianlong, Jiaqing, Daoguang, etc. they visited Laolongtou to enjoy the sea and to drink and write poems on their way to the northeast to pay homage to their ancestors or after visiting their folks.

In 1900, the eight-power allied force invaded China. After landing near Shanhaiguan, they burnt down Chenghai Tower and Ninghai City. The Laolongtou Great Wall built in the Ming Dynasty does not exist any more, but on its old site, now a new Laolongtou Great Wall was rebuilt. Ninghai and Chenghai Tower have been repaired too for sightseeing.

Jiaoshan Great Wall （角山长城）

It lies 3 kilometers north of Shanhaiguan. The mountain summit is of 519 meters in height and with its shape like a dragon horn, hence the name Jiaoshan, meaning in Chinese horn mountain. This part of the Great Wall is the first segment on mountainous areas after the Great Wall finishes its winding on the seashore. Therefore, Jiaoshan is also called The No.1 Mountain on the Great Wall.

From No.10 Terrace of Hanmen the Jiaoshan Great Wall snakes on the mountains for over four kilometers, with the shape of a bent line. Many watchtowers and castles stand on this Great Wall with different sizes and forms, constituting a firm defensive work. Connected closely together, a defense network that the enemy arrows cannot reach and the enemy cavalry dare not approach is completed.

Shanhaiguan Great Wall Museum （山海关长城博物馆）

It lies at the southern side of the famous Shanhaiguan Tower called the No.1 Pass in the world. A complex of ancient style buildings occupies 1.21-hectare land, with a floor area of 2,248 square meters. Under the eave of the main exhibition hall a golden character tablet written by the late Chairman, Li Xiannian, is hanged. On 1 July 1991, the Museum was open to tourists.

The contents of the Museum is rich, with a collection of the origin, forms, sizes, related historical figures, wars, etc. about the Great Wall, especially the architecture and military role of the most important part of the Great Wall, Shanhaiguan Great Wall. Many invaluable cultural relics and models, sculptures, and other data about the Great Wall are stored in it. The large-scale audio-video Shanhaiguan Cultural Relics Sand Table vividly shows the historical charm and modern glamour of Shanhaiguan. This museum is the largest among its peers in China that focus on the Great Wall as theme, enjoying a worldwide fame.

Banchang Ravine Great Wall （板厂峪长城）

It spreads the border areas of northern Funing County, Hebei Province, with a length of about 15 kilometers.

The geographic location is critical. The construction is great, with many watchtowers forming a network and the highest watchtower on a summit of 800 meters. In its over fifty watchtowers, more than thirty are in good conditions. More than ten Great Wall boundary markers are rare in the existing Ming Great Wall. Especially the Ming Great Wall here is varying in construction forms. It comprehensively exhibits the unique charm of the Ming Great Wall defensive work by its complete military facilities such as fire signal towers, watchtowers, castles, etc.

Dongjiakou Great Wall （董家口长城）

Dongjiakou Village lies in the northeastern mountainous area of Zhucaoying Town, Funing County, consisting of three natural villages and 122 households.

The Dongjiakou Great Wall was first built as second-class frontier wall in the fourteenth year of Hongwu of Ming (1381) and then as first-class in the fifth year of Longqing (1571). It snakes on Shiti Mountain, Mao Mountain, and Dalazi Mountain, with a total length of 8.9 kilometers, two passes, 31 watchtowers, 18 fighting terraces, and 14 fire signal towers. Three castles were built: Pochengzi, Damaoshan, and Dongjiakou. The Dongjiakou Ming Great Wall has a history of 621 years and is the best conserved Ming Great Wall. The villagers in Dongjiakou are the only offsprings of the people who built and guarded the Great Wall. Its geographic position is very important, with rich vegetation and animals. The varying forms of the structures, the complete military facilities for defense, and the coordinated fire signal towers, watchtowers, fighting terraces, and passes comprehensively exhibit the unique philosophy of the Ming Great Wall defense work.

Baiyang Ravine Great Wall （白羊峪长城）

It winds on the southern ridges of Yanshan Mountain 20 kilometers north of Qian'an, Hebei Province. It starts from the marble Great Wall in the east on Dazhuangbei Mountain, and then it runs to Laoduntai, Sidaogou, in the west, with a total length of 7,000 meters. It was built in the seventh year of Tianbao of Northern Qi (556) and called chong for its topographic position, meaning a critical point in Chinese. In the history, it has been consolidated for many times. After the movement of the capital to Beijing in the nineteenth year of Yongle of Ming (1421), the Jizhen Great Wall from Shanhaiguan to Juyongguan shouldered the heavy task of protecting the capital. In the end of the first year of Longqing (1567), the famous general in fighting the Japanese, Qi Jiguang, was appointed the commander of Jizhen, stationed at Santunying. Three vice commander were appointed, with each in charge of four generals. These generals were each in charge of a number of subordinate officers. Standing troops were stationed at Baiyang Ravine, supervised militarily by a general under the command of one of the vice commanders. During the sixteen years when Qi Jiguang was commander of Jizhen, he stressed on defensive projects. On the one hand, he built thick walls at critical positions; on the other, he built hollow watchtowers on the Great Wall for stationed troops. By constant drilling, his men became the most prominent among the nine towns. Therefore, the Jizhen Great Wall became the best part of the Great Wall.

Baiyang Ravine is also called Baiyangguan Pass. While Lengkou is famous for its difficult topographic position, Baiyangguan is known for its firm pass. Together, they are called firm and difficult passes. It integrates water gates, castles, fire signal towers, walls, watchtowers, slopes, ditches, etc. to make a complete military defense network.

Hongshankou （洪山口城）

It is a famous pass on the Great Wall. In the Ming Dynasty, it exerted critical role in defending against the declining Mongolians. During the later years of Ming and the beginning years of Qing, it became a pass for warding off the Qing troops.

It was established probably around the Warring States Period. In August of the first year of Hongwu of Ming Emperor Taizu (1368), great general, Xu Da, set up six military regions including Yanshan, and Hongshankou was one of them. In the fifteenth year of Hongwu, Ming government stationed troops at more than 200 passes including One Piece of Stone Pass and Hongshankou.

Hongshankou was built to defend against the remnant Yuan troops. Its disposition was like a triangle to utilize the topography. Viewed from the Great Wall on the hills to the north of the city, it resembled very much an official hat of the Ming Dynasty, therefore it was called also Official Hat City. On all its sides there are mountains and hills. To the north of the pass lies the Great Wall. Hongshankou Pass locates between two mountains and therefore forms a very difficult pass to break through.

Xifengkou （喜峰口）

It lies 50 kilometers to the northwest of Qianxi County, Hebei Province, one of the 32 key passes built by great general, Xu Da, in the beginning years of Hongwu of the Ming Dynasty on the Yan ridges. Later, every Emperor of the Ming Dynasty continued to repair the defense work at Xifengkou. In July of the third year of Jingtai (1452), a 13-meter high Zhenyuan Tower was built on top of the pass gate.

The construction of Xifengkou Pass is very unique. It has three passes that are connected by solid brick walls on stone foundations. At the six junctions of the walls, hollow watchtowers are designed to station troops. The western wall is connected with the main body of the Great Wall.

In 1976, after the river closure of the Panjiakou Reservoir of the national key water resource project, Diversion of the River Luan to Tianjin, Xifengkou and its pass were all immerged in the reservoir. When tourists come to the beautiful reservoir resort, they can enjoy the scenery of little three gorges as well as the charm of the Great Wall that winds on the surrounding mountains and hills.

Huangyaguan Pass （黄崖关）

Huangyaguan Great Wall was first built in the tenth year of Tianbao of Northern Qi (559). During the years of Yongle of the Ming Dynasty, a major repair was conducted on the basis of the Northern Qi Great Wall, making it a key pass on the Jizhen Ming Great Wall. Ming poet, Li Panlong, wrote a famous poem singing praise of the Huangyaguan Great Wall.

When repairing Huangyaguan, the Ming Dynasty extended the walls from the pass

and built Zhenguan and Shuiguan. The eastern side of the pass has many precipitous cliffs, with brown rocks. In the sunshine of sunset, the mountains exhibit a golden color, hence the name Huangyaguan, meaning in Chinese Yellow Cliff Pass. In recent years, from Wangmaoding cliff west of Huangyaguan to Banlagang Mountain cliff at Taipingzhai a length of 3,025 meters of the wall was repaired, with 25 towers, 1 Bagua pass, 1 Zhenguan tower, and 1 Taipingzhai castle. Meanwhile, in the Qian sec-

tion of the Bagua City a relatively large modern tablets collection in Northern China Huangyaguan Tablets Collection, was established.

The Huangyaguan Great Wall is 28 kilometers north of Ji County, Tianjin, with convenient traffic. Now it has become a good place for tourism.

Simatai （司马台）

The Simatai Great Wall lies to the northeast of Miyun County, Beijing, with a distance of 120 kilometers from Beijing. It begins from Wangjing Tower in the east and is connected with Jinshan Ridge Great Wall in the west. It was first built during the years of Hongwu of the Ming Dynasty with firm castles. In the years of Wanli, brick and stonewalls and watchtowers were built.

The topography of this part of the Great Wall is very difficult for access. To adapt to this situation, varying forms of walls were built with different sizes. The walls include single-sided, double-sided, brick, stone, and mixture of brick and stone ones. Barrier walls were also built to facilitate attack and defense. On the foot of the

A bird's eye view of Simatai Great Wall
鸟瞰司马台长城

mountains the Great Wall has a width of about 5 to 6 meters, while on top of the summit cliffs the width is only the length of two bricks. This two-brick width Great Wall is unique to Simatai Great Wall, called Heaven Bridge. Some parts of it were built on steep ridges with an angle of almost ninety degrees, rendering climbing extremely difficult. The heaven bridge can accommodate only a single person in climbing. The single-sided wall on top of the precipitous cliffs with many arrow-loops and wall for cover make it very difficult to break through for enemies, similar to a walk in many ways. In areas with even topography the walls are thick and high. An outer wall was designed inside the wall, without battlement but with densely designed arrow-loops.

There are two famous watchtowers on the Simatai Great Wall: Wangjing Tower and Xiannu Tower. Wangjing Tower was built on top of a summit that has an elevation of nearly one thousand meters. It is said that under the clear sky after rain people can see Beijing on the Tower. At night, Beijing's gleaming lights can be seen too. Wangjing in Chinese means looking at the capital. Xiannu Tower lies to the west of Wangjing Tower. The route to it is very difficult, with the steep cliffs. This tower is very beautiful with its white marble arches and double-lotus reliefs.

A snowy scene of Xiannu Tower

仙女楼雪景

Xiannü Tower Great Wall
仙女楼长城

A panoramic view of Jinshan Ridge Great Wall looking form Simatai
司马望金山

Jinshan Ridge　　（金山岭）

The Jinshan Ridge Great Wall lies at the junction of Miyun, Beijing, and Luanping, Hebei. It acquired its name because it was built on the great and small Jin Mountains. This part of the Great Wall is exemplary of the whole Great Wall.

One of the features is its densely designed watchtowers. Generally, every 100 meters a watchtower was built. In complex topographies, every fifty meters there is a watchtower.

Among the famous watchtowers there are Jiangjun, Xiannu, Wangjing, Taochun, Huding, etc. Some of them were cleverly designed, with no access from either side, but only a passage through arches inside the wall by using a small ladder. This design was for the purpose of preventing the enemy entrance inside the wall. Among the many watchtowers, there is one with white marble doorframes with delicate carvings and reliefs. It is said to be the office of Jizhen commander, Qi Jiguang. The watchtowers on the Jinshan Ridge Great Wall are classified according to the number of arrow-loops, such as three-loop tower, four-loop tower, and five-loop tower. If classified according to the roof forms,

here are flat roof, saddle roof, dome roof, pyramid roof, octagon roof, etc.

The excellent architecture plus its critical geographic position make it an ideal place to enjoy the northern China scenery. During the many repairs, archaeologists found many valuable cultural relics. Bricks with characters and tablets are numerous in number. They are invaluable artifacts for modern people to understand the construction of the Ming Great Wall.

Lesser Jinshan Tower Great Wall

小金山楼长城

Kylin Screen at Jinshan Ridge Great Wall
金山岭长城麒麟影壁

Jinshan Ridge Great Wall
金山岭长城

Gubeikou （古北口）

It locates in the north of Miyun County, Beijing, a traffic hub connecting the south and north of Yan Ridges, with Panlong and Wohu Mountains at its back, Qingfeng and Diecui Mountains in the south, and the Chao River crossing the pass from south to north. The main body of the Great Wall links Panlong and Wohu mountains into a line.

Its construction period, according to historical records, should be in the Tang Dynasty. After the Ming overthrew the Yuan Dynasty, Emperor Taizu, Zhu Yuanzhang, ordered Xu Da to build the Great Wall and Gubeikou was among the first passes to be built by this general. Its pass city locates on top of a summit, covering Dongguanmen in the east, the Chao River in the west, Dakai Ridge in the south, and Gaoshanjian in the north. The city was called Yingcheng, with a circumference of about two kilometers and eastern, northern, and southern gates.

It is one of the passes on the Great Wall that has seen numerous wars. The famous Jiajing Gengxu Incident in the Ming history selected here as the main battlefield. Afterwards, the Ming government strengthened the defense at Gubeikou by appointing more generals and sending more troops.

Gubeikou has now become an important sightseeing resort on route of Beijing to Chengde Mountain Resort.

Gubeikou Great Wall
古北口长城

Remnants of Gubeikou Great Wall
古北口残长城

The Mutian Ravine Great Wall locates to the north of Sanduhe Town, Huairou District, Beijing, with a distance of 70 kilometers from Beijing. It connects Gubeikou in the east

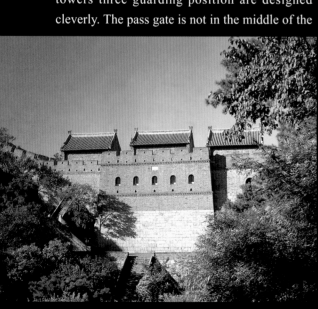

and Juyongguan in the west, one of the ten great landscapes of Beijing, with the title of imposing pass on precipitous ridges.

The Mutian Ravine Great Wall was built on the basis of the Northern Qi Great Wall by the Ming authorities. It consists mainly of walls, watchtowers, passes, and fire signal towers, constituting a complete, firm military defense system.

Its construction and facilities have many unique features: strange Zhengguan tower. The gate of the pass consists of three hollow watchtowers that are connected with each other. The towers on both sides are small, with narrow rooms, while the middle hall is spacious and imposing. On top of the three watchtowers three guarding position are designed cleverly. The pass gate is not in the middle of the wall, but is designed to use left and right passageways to access from steps. This strange architecture coupled with the Great Wall's double side arrow-loops is very rare in other segments of the Great Wall. The wall is firm and the watchtowers difficult to access. Generally, the major wall has a base width of six meters and a top width of four meters and a height of eight meters. Both sides of the wall are covered by thirteen layers of granite slabs, making the wall extremely firm. The top width of the wall is smaller than average Great Wall, but with its varying forms, more military value and tourist worth are generated. Despite sizes, the watchtowers are designed into two stories, with a triangle or circular passageway in between for stationing troops or supplies. Arrow-loops are designed alongside the passageways to defend against the enemy. On top of the towers, a circle of shooting points is built, with some watchtowers built with arrow towers.

The famous resorts and sites of the Mutian Ravine Great Wall include: Niujiaobian, Jiankou, Yingfeidaoyang, and Nine-loop Tower.

Mutian Ravine Great Wall after Snow

慕田峪雪景

Mutian Ravine Great Wall
慕田峪长城

Jiankou （箭扣）

It lies on the southeastern and northern walls of Niujiaobian that are built on cliffs of tens of *zhang* in height. From Jiankou watchtower westwards, due to the narrowness of the place for building walls, only an arrow-loop-like wall was built, called single side. At a special position that offers no support for building a wall, two iron bars had to be used to connect two rocks in order that the wall could be built continuously.

Jiankou Great Wall in winter

箭扣之冬

Niujiaobian section of Jiankou Great Wall
慕田峪长城牛犄角边

Snowy scene of Jiankou Great Wall

银装箭扣

Yingfeidaoyang （鹰飞倒仰）

It lies to the southwest of an old pond in Xizhazi Village. The wall was built alongside the steep cliff like a ladder to the heaven. Even the eagles have to climb on its back to pass this wall, hence the name, meaning literally, eagle flying belly up. From it to the northern tower of Taoyukou, there are other difficult to access places such as edging one's way, urn mouth, falling into sea, stone gate, etc. along the route.

Beijing Knot （北京结）

It lies between east longitude 116° 29' 38.8'' and north latitude 40° 27' 45''. The main body of the Great Wall coming from Shanhaiguan divides into two from it. One runs westwards to connect Juyongguan Pass and Zijingguan Pass, forming the inner Great Wall. The other winds northwestwards to connect Dushikou and Zhangjiakou, forming the outer Great Wall. Here the three brick and stone Great Walls meet at the summit of Huoshi Mountain, forming unique scenery of the Great Wall.

Bohai Barracks （渤海所城）

It locates 25 kilometers northwest of Huairou, Beijing, built in the thirty-second year of Jiajing of the Ming Dynasty. It is encircled by mountains at all sides, forming a small basin. The city lies in the north of the basin at the foot of the Northern Hill. The city wall has a length of 1,467 meters, a width of four meters, and a height of 6.8 meters. The wall was built solely with stones. The city has an area of 1.2096 million square meters. There are four gates, with the northern one blocked; on the board of the southern inner gate "Bohai City" is inscribed, while on the board of the southern outer gate "Huanghua Road". The 18-meter wide street facing the four directions formed a spacious crossroad. In the middle of the street a row of stone slabs were inset, with hundreds of ancient Chinese scholar trees. To the west of the city center locates the then military commander's office.

Bohai Barracks was also an important defense work for the royal mausoleums of the Ming Dynasty. Originally only Huanghua Road military station was in charge of the protection of the back door of the mausoleums. In the thirty-second year of Jiajing (1553), a general was transferred to Bohai Barracks in order to ward off the enemy in the east and protect the mausoleums in the west.

Huanghua City Great Wall （黄花城长城）

It lies in the northwest of Jiuduhe Town, Huairou District, Beijing, built between the second year of Yongle of Ming and the twentieth year of Wanli of Ming (1404-1592). It starts in the west from the summit of Wangquanyu at the border with Yanqing County, and ends at the cliff of Shibadeng in the east. The total length is 12.4 kilometers, with forty hollow watchtowers, nine solid watchtowers, five wall terraces, and eight passes.

The part of the Great Wall features steep topography and fine workmanship. To the west of Shihuyu the wall was built with stone slabs; to its east, however, the wall was built with stone foundation and brick wall. According to *Probe into Old Legends*: Huanghua Town is the north-

ern gate of the capital. It connects Shanhaiguan in the east and Juyongguan in the west. Its northern side is oceans. Therefore, its strategic position is very great. The watchtowers here use the topography cleverly, with many different forms. Especially Zhuangdaokou area, the watchtowers are densely disposed. The smallest interval is only sixty meters and the biggest not exceeding 105 meters. The pass is well equipped in facilities, with three passes in turn, i.e. the first, second, and the third pass. By such design, a complete defense work is created.

Juyongguan Pass （居庸关）

It is one of the most famous passes on the Great Wall, being the barrier to the northwest of Beijing since the ancient times. In recent years, it has become a famous Great Wall resort after many repairs and developments.

Among the famous Eight Taihang Passes, Juyongguan is the eighth, i.e. the Jundu Pass controlling the access to Jundu Mountain. In its long history, although an important military base, it has changed for many times its name. In the Three Kingdoms Period, it was called Xiguan, meaning the western pass. In the times of Northern Qi, it changed to Nakuanguan. During the Tang Dynasty, it first was called Jimenguan, and then changed to Junduguan. Since Liao times through to Later Jin, Yuan, Ming, Qing, and modern times, it has been called Juyongguan.

In the third year of Hongwu (1370), to defeat the counterattack of the remnant Mongolian forces, Zhu Yuanzhang ordered Xu Da to build Juyongguan Pass, with an area that was the largest compared with that of the previous dynasties. After its construction, a military office was set up there. In the third year of Yongle, the role of the pass was promoted to command five similar units. After its initial building in the beginning years of Hongwu of the Ming Dynasty, the later emperors of the Ming Dynasty did not stop repairing and consolidating it, especially in the beginning years of Jingtai. After the Tumubao Incident, the then defense minister, Yu Qian, suggested: due to its critical position, more force should be sent to guard Juyongguan in order to better protect the capital; Wang Rong should be sent to station and repair Juyongguan Pass. On the remaining southern gate tablet there is a sentence reading made in an auspicious day in August of the fifth year of Jingtai.

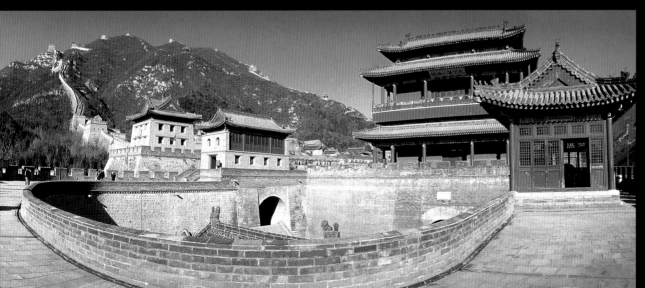

Cloud-Terrace of Juyongguan Pass
居庸关云台

Juyongguan Great Wall
居庸关长城

Bada Ridge （八达岭）

It is the outer part of Juyongguan, and because of its location to the north of Juyongguan, it is also called Beikou, meaning North Mouth. Because from there southwards people can travel to Beijing, northwards, Yanqing, westwards, Xuanhua, Zhangjiakou and Datong, therefore it acquired its name, literally meaning the ridge from which you can reach eight directions. It was an important barrier in the Ming Dynasty. Ancient people said: the difficulty for access does not lie at Juyongguan Pass, but at Bada Ridge.

It is a small pass, having eastern and western gates. On the eastern gate there is a stone tablet saying Juyongguan's outer town; on the western gate the stone tablet reads the key to the northern gate. The distance between the two gates is sixty-four meters. Bada Ridge was first built in the eighteenth year of Hongzhi of the Ming Dynasty (1505). The wall was built mostly with giant granite slabs and therefore very firm. Bricks were

used to cover the top of the wall. The height of the wall varies according to the height of the mountains and hills, with an average height of about 8.5 meters, a foundation width of 6.5 meters, and a top width of 5.7 meters. On the wall five horses can run or ten soldiers can march shoulder by shoulder. Inside the top of the wall a short wall was added, while outside it arrow-loops were designed. Every 250-500 meters there is a hollow watchtower. In 1953, the government granted a fund to repair the two gates of Bada Ridge. In 1958, the state government decided to develop and repair the Bada

Ridge Great Wall. From then on, Bada Ridge gradually becomes a tourist resort of world fame.

Now, whenever people mention the Great Wall they think of Bada Ridge. The Great Wall has become a symbol of the Chinese peoples, and the Bada Ridge Great Wall has become a spokesman for the whole Great Wall. Many heads of states climbed the Bada Ridge Great Wall during their visit to China. According to statistics, so far 388 heads of states have visited the Bada Ridge Great Wall.

Bada Ridge Great Wall
八达岭长城

Bada Ridge Great Wall in autumn
八达岭秋色

Bada Ridge Great Wall
八达岭长城

Bada Ridge Great Wall
八达岭长城

Bada Ridge Great Wall Museum （八达岭长城博物馆）

It locates on the southern slope of Guntiangou outside the western gate of Bada Ridge Pass, with a floor area of four thousand square meters. Its look is similar to a terrace-like structure called Duntai of the Great Wall, with arrow-loops, it agrees with the remote Great Wall completely. It has four exhibition halls: a prelude hall for exhibiting the overall charm of the Chinese Great Wall; No.2 hall is devoted to exhibiting the Great Wall previous to the Ming Dynasty; No.3 hall shows the Ming Great Wall; No. 4 holds a collection of paintings and calligraphy works with the theme of Loving China, Repairing the Great Wall. The Museum helps visitors to understand the history and charm of the Great Wall.

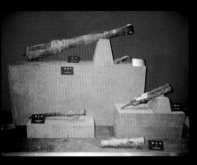

Dushikou （独石口）

It locates in the north of Chicheng, Hebei Province, an important pass on Xuanfuzhen Ming Great Wall. Because there is a monolith at the location of the pass, hence the name, literally meaning sole stone mouth. On this rock there are two groups of characters inscribed, respectively, outstanding sole glamour and a rock flying from afar.

Its geographic position is very important, called by former military strategists: throat to Shanggu and right arm of the capital.

It was built in the fifth year of Xuande of the Ming Dynasty with rammed loess. During the Tumubo Incident in the fourteenth year of Zhengtong (1449) it was broken by the Oirat tribes of the Mongolians and suffered great damages. Afterwards, several repairs were conducted. In the tenth year of Wanli (1582), the governor of Zhili Province, Sun Jiagan organized a large-scale repair of the desolated Dushicheng.

During the Anti-Japanese War, famous national hero and general, Ji Hongchang, summoned a mobilization meeting at Dushikou before he led his men to engage the Japanese. He wrote on a stone tablet Driving the enemy and restoring peace to the frontiers to inspire his men.

Ancient Xuanhua City （宣化古城）

It locates in Xuanhua District, Zhangjiakou. The ancient city was first built in the Tang Dynasty. In the twenty-seventh year of Hongwu of the Ming Dynasty (1394), it was expanded and covered with bricks. The city wall is square in shape, with each side having a length of over three kilometers. The wall has an overall height of 11.7 meters with the wall height of 9.3 meters and the arrow-loop height of 2.3 meters. Seven gates were built around the wall: in the south there are Changping, Xuande and Cheng'an gates; in the north, Guangling and Gaoyuan gates; in the east, Ding'an gate; and in the west, Taixin gate. Outside the gates are passes with circular structure called Wencheng. Outside the Wencheng there are crescent city, with corner towers on the four corners. Outside it there are ditches, moats, and drawbridges. The disposition resembles Beijing city in many ways. It is now among the few Ming cities that have earthen walls.

The southern wall middle gate, Changping gate, has a tower called Gongji, or Zhugeng. The tower is 14 meters in height with two stories. It was built on top of a 9-meter high archway that is south northward, forming a central line of Xuanhua City together with the northern Qingyuan and Zhenshuo Towers.

The ancient walls and Gongji Tower are both provincial key cultural relics protection units of Hebei.

Zhangjiakou （张家口）

It lies at the northern verge of the Xuanhua Basin between Taihang and Yanshan

Mountains. Having the title of the capital's northern gateway, it has always been a traffic hub from North China to Inner Mongolia. It is also an important pass on the Great Wall.

According to historical records, in the fourth year of Xuande (1429), the Ming Dynasty built Zhangjiakou Castle. The castle is square in shape with a circumference of about 2 kilometers and a height of 3 *zhang* and 3 *chi*. There were gates on the eastern and southern sides, with the eastern gate called Yongzhen and the southern one called Cheng'en.

In Zhangjiakou, Dajingmen is connected with the Great Wall. Like two giant arms, the Great Wall extends on the eastern and western sides of Dajingmen along the mountainous topography on Eastern and Western Taiping mountains. Dajingmen was a passageway opened on the Ming Zhangjiakou Great Wall in the first year of Shunzhi of the Qing Dynasty (1644). It was built with stone slabs as foundation and brick arches. The gate wall has a height of 12 meters, a base length of 13 meters, and a width of 9 meters. The outer side of the arch has a height of 5.4 meters and a width of 6 meters. There are two wooden doors covered in iron sheet. On top of the gate there is a tablet written with four characters, great mountains and rivers, by the governor of Chahar Province, Gao Weiyue. After several major repairs, Dajingmen has become a famous tourist resort.

Datong （大同）

It locates in the north of Shanxi Province at the junction triangle of Shanxi, Hebei, and Inner Mongolia, an important military position in the northern China. With the title of northern key, it has been the most contended area by the military strategists in the history.

Datong in the Ming Dynasty was a key position on the border, providing a barrier to the capital. It was one of the nine towns on the Great Wall. The military commander was stationed at today's Datong, in charge of the Great Wall from Yajiao Mountain in the west to Zhenkoutai in the east. In the fifth year of Hongwu of the Ming Dynasty (1372),

great general Xu Da led people to expand the Datong city and to make it firmer. The city is square in shape, with the side length of 1.5 kilometers, a circumference of 6.5 kilometers and an area of 2.63 square kilometers. The wall was made of rammed earth and covered with bricks. Outside the wall there are moat and ditches. Inside the wall the city was designed with crossroads as backbone, connecting the four gates in the east, west, south, and north. Outside the wall, roads connecting the suburbs and the routes to the Great Wall were built. The crossroads in the city also had a function of dividing the living blocks and connecting small lanes. The junctions of the crossroads formed the center of the city, with archway towers at four sides. A drum tower was also built in the southern street, south of pailou; in the eastern and western streets Taiyi Tower and a bell tower were built. The three towers are well coordinated and thus forming a very good scene.

Pianguan Pass （偏关）

The Pianguan Pass locates at today's Pianguan County, Shanxi Province, connecting Guancen Mountain in the east, the Yellow River in the west, Inner Mongolia in the north, and Yanmen and Ningwu in the south. It has been a most contended place for military strategists and for stationing troops since the ancient times.

From the Five Dynasties to the Song Dynasty, Piantouzhai had been located here. In the Jin Dynasty, it used this name too. During the Yuan Dynasty, it changed its name to Piantouguan. However, the then location was on Yuhuangliang Ridge in the west of today's Pianguan County. In the twenty-third year of Hongwu of Ming (1390), the western military commander, Zhang Xian, set up Pianguan military region and began to build a new city. After several expansions occurred in the years of Xuande, Tianshun, Chenghua, and Hongzhi, the city finally had the size of today, with a circumference of about 2.5 kilometers, a wall height of 11.7 meters, and three gates in the east, west, and south.

There is a hollow brick pagoda on Eastern Hill outside the Pianguan City, called Wenbilingxiao Pagoda, which was built in the years of Tianqi of the Ming Dynasty. When first finished, the pagoda had seven stories. In the eighth year of Chongzhen of the Ming Dynasty (1635), another four stories were added, making the total height increase to 30 meters. Now the pagoda has been regarded as the symbol of Pianguan.

Ningwuguan Pass （宁武关）

It lies at the southern slope of Guancen Mountain, with the pass on Huagai Mountain in the north, controlling Fenghuang Mountain in the south. The River Hui runs eastwards from the south of the city. The two wings of the city were built alongside the river, making the strategic position extremely important.

Because of its location to the north of Fenghuang Mountain, it has been also called Fenghuang City since the ancient times. It was first built in the first year of Jingtai of the Ming Dynasty (1450) and had been repaired in the years of Chenghua, Zhengde, and Longqing of the Ming Dynasty. After the repair in the second year of Chenghua (1466), the city had a circumference of about 2 kilometers, a base width of 15 meters, a top width of 7.5 meters, a wall height of 10 meters, and eastern, western, and southern gates. In the eleventh year of Hongzhi (1498), the city was expanded to have a circumference of 3.5 kilometers. The city wall was increased in height by 1.5 meters and a northern gate was opened. The wall then was still of rammed loess. The brick wall was added in the thirty-fourth year of Wanli (1606). During the years of Wanli, eastern and western gate towers were also added. On the summit of Huagai Mountain north of the city a protective battlement was added, with a three-story tower called Huagai Tower. In the last years of the Ming Dynasty, Li Zicheng overthrew Emperor Chongzhen. He engaged the Ming commander, Zhou Yuji, at Ningwuguan Pass, and cleared his last barrier to Beijing.

Yanmenguan Pass （雁门关）

It locates on the summit of the major mountain of Hengshan Mountain in Dai County, Shanxi Province, 400 kilometers from western Beijing. It is known for its difficult access.

The architecture is great, with a circumference of about 1 kilometer and a wall height of over 6 meters. The wall was built with bricks on stone foundation, with rammed earth in between the wall. The city has three gates, i.e. eastern gate, western gate, and little northern gate. Now only the eastern and western gates are remaining, while the little northern gate has been demolished. There is a stone tablet on each gate, reading respectively, natural barrier and great topography, describing its critical position in military defense. A gate tower was established on each gate, which was burnt down by the invading Japanese troops in the Anti-Japanese War. The damaged little northern gate

had a stone tablet saying Yanmenguan Pass with two brick couplets, which were all demolished together with the gate. Along the Yanmenguan area, the topography is mountainous. The old inner Great Wall snakes on top of the mountains and hills like a jade belt that connects the summits and peaks. On top of the mountains fire signal towers are many in number, forming an effective defense work in combination with castles, towers, watchtowers, and other facilities on the Great Wall.

Today, it has become a new tourist resort that has a collection of northern China's frontier culture, pass culture, war culture, and military culture.

Bianjing Tower （边靖楼）

It is in city of Dai County, Shanxi Province, called by local people Drum Tower. Its look is imposing with high foundation and delicate frameworks. After hundreds of years of weathering and many earthquakes, it remained untouched and in good conditions. The southern and northern archways form a passageway through the tower, with a foundation height of 13 meters, a length of 43 meters, and a width of 33 meters. The tower has a height of 26 meters and is divided into three stories, with a gabled roof. Inside the tower, the width can accommodate seven rooms and the depth five. Cloisters are designed around the tower. On the third story, a flat base is added to the railings. The tower was first built in the seventh year of Hongwu of the Ming Dynasty (1374) and was rebuilt after burning down in the seventh year of Chenghua of the Ming Dynasty (1471) with added foundations. Three giant tablets are hanged on the tower, saying, respectively, reaching four directions, controlling the three passes, and the number one tower at Yanmen.

Pingxingguan Pass （平型关）

It is an important pass on the part of the Great Wall in Shanxi Province. Originally, the name meant bottle-shaped pass. Since the ancient times, it controls Zijingguan in the east, Yanmenguan in the west and has been stressed by many military strategists. As early as Northern Qi and Northern Zhou times, the authorities began to build pass and Great Wall there. In Northern Song times, a bottle-shaped castle was set up there.

In the sixth year of Zhengde of the Ming Dynasty (1511), when the Great Wall was built in large scale, a pass and a segment of the Great Wall were built there, making it an important position at the wing of Yanmenguan Pass. The Pingxingguan Pass is located 1 kilometer northeast of Pingxingguan Village, Hengjian Town, Fanshi County, on a slow slope between two mountains. At the mouth of the pass a small city was built, which has been damaged now. An archway is remaining, with a tablet on it, reading Pingxingguan Pass. According to the local people, on top of the pass terrace there was a single-story gate tower with three rooms, which in early years was flooded by storms. The present gate was rebuilt. On 25 September 1937, the 115th Division of the Eighth Route Army ambushed the Japanese and won the first victory after the Army made expedition into North China.

Niangziguan Pass （娘子关）

It locates in the northeast of Pingding County, Shanxi Province, which is an important pass on the Taihang Great Wall. The pass was built on top of a cliff, very difficult to access from below. The present pass city was built in the twenty-first year of Jiajing of the Ming Dynasty (1542). There are two gates, eastern and southern gates. The eastern gate is an archway made of bricks, with a stone tablet reading Zhili Niangziguan Pass. The southern gate was built with stones with a stone tablet on the archway, reading bar-

ler to the capital. The two tablets show that then the eastern gate was facing inwards while the southern gate was used to face the enemy. Outside the southern gate there is only a steep slope of nearly 25 degree for access to the city.

A tower was built on the southern wall terrace south of the pass, with four granite columns at the front gallery and four couplets with distinguishable Chinese characters.

Guguan Pass （固关）

It locates in Pingding County, Shanxi Province. 6 kilometers south of Niangziguan Pass, there is the remains of the Guguan Pass (old site). According to *Da Qing Yi Tong Zhi (Great Qing Unification Records)*: in the second year of Zhengtong of the Ming Dynasty (1437), a pass was built to station troops.

The Guguan Pass (new site) lies 2.5 kilometers south of the old site. The brick arch-

way of the new site is still in good conditions, with a stone carving on top of the archway, reading Guguan Pass. On the wall, there is a record tablet about the rebuilding of the Guguan Pass in the first year of Shunzhi of the Qing Dynasty (1644). The northern gate and the water gate of Guguan Pass were dismantled in 1981 by the Guguan Village Commune. It is said that the water gate was very unique in construction, with fine animal sculptures on the two sides of the water gate archway. With Guguan as center, a segment of wall was built on western and on southern directions to strengthen the defense.

Zijingguan Pass （紫荆关）

It is an important pass on the Great Wall. Locating at a place 45 kilometers away from Yi County, Hebei Province, it acquired its name from its position on Zijing Ridge.

The pass relies on Wanren Mountain in the east and faces Xiniu Mountain in the west. The wide riverbed of the River Juma crosses the northern side of the Great Wall. The geographic location is very critical.

Zijingguan Pass is among the few in the hundreds of

passes on the Great Wall that have long history. From Qin to Song, many dynasties have stationed troops to guard this location. It therefore acquired the title of the number one great pass in the area south of the capital. Due to its important military significance, Zijingguan Pass has been the place focused by military strategists in the history. According to statistics, the wars happened there are hundreds in number. Therefore, it occupies an important position in Chinese war history. It has nine gates, four water gates, with connected inner and outer walls. Unwary enemies are easily lost in its labyrinth network and suffer their doom.

Daomaguan Pass （倒马关）

It lies in the northwest of Tang County, Hebei Province. The name means falling horses, because the horses often fall there due to its difficult topography. Its history can be traced to very early times. In *Zhan Guo Ce (Records of the Warring States)*, it was called Hongshangguan, while in the Han Dynasty, Changshanguan. However, the present records about the pass are all from the Ming Dynasty. Due to its special location, it has very high military value in the history.

Together with Juyongguan and Zijingguan, the three passes are called collectively the Inner Three Passes. Its construction is very unique, too, with a half in the valley and the other half on the mountain. From three sides, i.e. the west, north, and east, the River Tang flows

around it. The mountains, rivers and pass form a perfect barrier to the enemy. The pass city has a circumference of 2.5 kilometers, a wall foundation width of 6 meters, a wall top width of 4 meters, and a height of 10 meters. The wall was with rammed loess covered by bricks and stones. The city has three gates. The eastern gate is called Juren; the western gate, Youyi; and the northern gate, Yiwu. One hundred paces away from the western gate there is another gate built with stone slabs. On the surrounding mountains, there are five stone terraces, now collapsed, with only half of one remaining.

Wulonggou Great Wall （乌龙沟长城）

This part of the Great Wall lies in the northeast of Laiyuan County, Baoding City, Hebei Province, with a total length of about 20 kilometers. It was under the command of Zijingguan Road, Qibaozhen, having five passes. The segment near Wulonggou is in better conditions, with most of the arrow-loops preserved perfectly. The watchtowers near Wulonggou are many. Averagely, every 400-500 meters there was built a watchtower, with about 40 of them in good conditions. 1 kilometer inside of the Great Wall locates the Wulonggou Castle, which is also in good conditions. The castle faces the mountain on one side, while the other three sides are near rivers. Therefore the location is very important. The castle is an irregular rectangle in shape, with the length from south to north being about 200 meters and that from east to west being about 150 meters.

The topography covered by this part of the Great Wall is mostly highly mountainous. The Great Wall winds like a giant dragon on the mountains. The verse mountains like sea and walls like dragons is no exaggeration. It is a prospect tourist resort along the Great Wall.

Ancient Yulin City （榆林古城）

It is now the location of Yulin City, Shaanxi Province. It was called Yuyang, too, controlling Yanshuo in the east, Ningxia in the west, Shaanxi in the south, and Hetao in the north.

According to historical records, Yulin Town was first established in the beginning years of Zhengtong of the Ming Dynasty. In the ninth year of Chenghua (1473), governor Yu Zijun repaired it and moved the official government from Suide to Yulin. Therefore, Yansui Town was also called Yulin City. Afterwards, Yulin City expanded in large scale for three times and the city became established. In the second year of Tongzhi of the Qing Dynasty (1863), sand dunes immerged the northern city; therefore, the northern wall was moved southwards, forming the present day Yulin City.

The topography of the city features high elevation in the east and low elevation in the west. The northeastern corner protrudes. The wall was rammed into shape and covered by bricks. The wall is 12 meters in height, with a base width of over 16 meters and a top width of 10 meters. The city has five gates that are all built with two-story gate towers that were all demolished. Today, the southern and eastern gate archway and Wencheng structure are remaining. Inside the city there is a Xinming Tower built in the years of Zhengde of the Ming

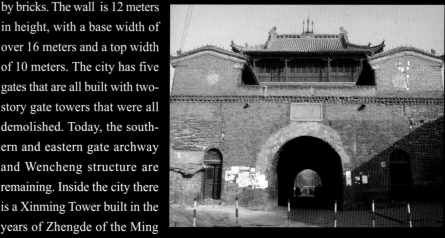

Dynasty, now a key cultural relics protection unit of Shaanxi Province.

Zhenbeitai （镇北台）

It is the largest terrace-like horse face on the Great Wall, locating on the Peak of Hong Mountain in Yulin City, Shaanxi Province. The eastern and western wings are connected with the Great Wall, controlling the exit and entrance from north to south. It was built in the thirty-fifth year of Wanli of the Ming Dynasty (1607). It was originally the sentry post set up by the local official of Yulin Town, Tu Zongjun, to protect the horse-trading at Hong Mountain. It relies on the Great Wall and embraces Hong Mountain. Standing on top of the horse face, a scope of tens of miles can be observed clearly. It is one of the famous passes on the Great Wall. In 1986, it was repaired to receive visitors.

It is square in shape, like a pagoda. The total height is over 30 meters and divided into four stories. On top of the fourth story a brick and wood sentry post was built that was demolished in the Qing Dynasty. The whole horse face is covered by bricks. On the second story an archway is opened facing the south, which is the only access to the top. A horizontal tablet reading towards the brightness was written by the

local official, Tu Zongjun. On top of it, the nearby scenery such as Hongshi Gorge can be seen. The city for receiving attributes from the Mongolians and other affairs is in the vicinity.

Yima Town （易马城）

It lies 5 kilometers west of Zhenbeitai in the north of Yulin City, on the part of the Great Wall east of Hongshi Gorge. In the fifth year of Longqing of the Ming Dynasty, Emperor Muzong made Altan Khan King Shunyi, and the khan's over 60 subordinates were also granted office or money. Following the event, alongside Datong, Xuanfu, Shanxi, Ningxia, Gansu, etc. many horse-trading markets were opened with the main purpose of transacting with Monan's Tumote, Erdos, etc. and Yima Town was one of the markets.

The plan of the city is like a quadrilateral with northwest side having a length of about 250 meters and the east to west side being 150 meters. The wall is in good conditions, with the eastern wall having a dimension of $250 \times 6 \times 6$ meter, the southern wall, $150 \times 10 \times 7$ meter, the western wall, $250 \times 4 \times 6$ meter, and the northern wall, $150 \times 4 \times 6$ meter. The remaining height of the rammed earth wall is between 6 and 7 meters and the width, 1 to 10 meters, with a rammed earth layer of 14 centimeters. It was the free trading market between the Chinese and the Mongolians, also a historical witness of the friendship and good will between the two peoples.

Hongshi Gorge （红石峡）

It locates on Hongshi Cliff 3 kilometers north of Yulin City, Shaanxi Province. The mountain gets its name because of the red rocks there. Hongshi in Chinese means red rock. The gorge has cliffs on its eastern and western sides, with a stream running in between with a thundering sound. The gorge is divided into southern and northern parts. The northern gorge has a Ming dam to cut off the Yuxi River; there are 44 grottoes in the southern gorge, with more than 200 stone, clay, or bronze Buddhist statues in it. On the eastern and western cliffs of the gorge, there are more than 160 stone carvings. Among them, the slogan the Mongolians and the Chinese are from the same family is very prominent. On the eastern cliff over 10 caves were made, called Xiongshan Temple. Along the steps, there are magnificent scenes such as Heaven's Gate and Earth's Gate. It is one of the Eight Yulin Scenes, with the splendid gorge in the sunshine. Now it has become a key tourist resort.

Jian'an Castle （建安堡）

It locates 1 kilometer southwest of Daheta Village, Daheta Town, Yuyang District, 2.5 kilometers away from Dabian, one of the 36 castles in Yansui Town in the Ming Dynasty. On the northern side of the castle is a river, on the west, a trench, and on the southeast, arable land. According to historical records, it was built in the tenth year of Chenghua of the Ming Dynasty (1474). In the thirty-fifth year of Wanli (1607) it was covered by brick. The city is rectangular in shape, with rammed earth walls covered with bricks. Fifteen Maqian walls surround it. There are three gates, i.e. the eastern, southern, and northern gates, which are all built with Wencheng structure. The southern gate wall is made of rammed earth covered with bricks with three archways. It has a width of 3.55 meters, a thickness of 9.9 meters, and a height of 4.32 meters. The northeastern half of the city is semicircle in shape, with corner towers on the southeastern, southwestern, and northwestern corners. A horse face was built on each of the eastern and western walls. Inside the city there are Niangniang Temple, Yanguang Temple, Bell and Drum Tower, etc. from the Ming and Qing dynasties. Now there are over 30 households living in the castle. The wall remains are in good conditions mostly.

In 1990, the local government of Yulin City listed Jian'an Castle as the city's key cultural relics protection unit.

Tongwan Town （统万城）

It lies in Baichengzi Village, Hongdunkou Town, Jingbian County, Shaanxi Province. It was originally the capital of Xia of the 16 states of the Northern Dynasties. According to historical records, in the first year of Yongsheng of Helianbobo (407), the Hun aristocrat, Helianbobo entitled himself the great Shanyu under the sky and dominated Shuomo area. In the first year of Fengxiang (413), he drove one hundred thousand people of various nationalities to build a capital to the north of the Shuofang River and to the south of the Li River. The capital was named Tongwan, meaning unifying the world's tens of thousands of states into one. Because of the white color of the earthen wall, it is also called Baichengzi, meaning in Chinese white city. The Town is very firm. The local people in laying their walls often fetch rectangular slabs of earth from the walls of the Tongwan Town, for the hardness of it is similar to bricks. Its remains now are invaded by the Mu-Us Desert, but the overall shape is there with most of the walls in good conditions.

Ancient Yinchuan City （银川古城）

The ancient Yinchuan City lies in the middle of the Ningxia Plain, now the capital of the Ningxia Hui Nationality Autonomous Region and one of the famous historical cities in China. About 1500 years ago, Great Xia established Yinhan City here and built Hebao Pagoda (Haibao Pagoda). In the Tang Dynasty, Huaiyuan Town was set up here. After the Western Xia established its capital, it was promoted as Xingqingfu, later changed to Zhongxingfu. When the Yuan Dynasty replaced Western Xia, it set up Ningxia Road there and changed Xingqingfu to Ningxiafu. In the Ming Dynasty, it is the military command office of Ningxia Town. The remains of the Western Xia are the main content of the Yinchuan tourism. The major tourist resorts include Western Xia mausoleums, Haibao Pagoda, Chengtian Temple's Pagoda, the Double Pagodas of Baisikou, Nanguan Mosque, together with rock paintings and Xiaogunzhongkou resort at Helan Mountain.

Sanguankou （三关口）

It locates in the middle of the Helan Mountain, 40 kilometers away from Yinchuan in the northeast. The road from Yinchuan to Bayan crosses Sanguankou.

According to *Jia Jing Ningxia Xin Zhi (New Jiajing Ningxia History)*: Sanguankou was built in 1540 by civilian official, Yang Shouli, and military commander, Ren Jie, having three passes from the east to the west. The first pass is the major one, connecting with the main body of the Great Wall in both the south and the north. The rammed earth wall was built on the northern hill, winding southwards from the pass.

The second pass lies 2.5 kilometers west of the first pass along the road. After the second pass and going westwards, the valley becomes narrower. After going about 2.5 kilometers, there is only a road between two steep cliffs, the third pass.

It is very rare for a series of three passes among the many passes on the Great Wall. This shows the military importance of Sanguankou in the ancient times. It controls the route into Ningxia Plain from Alashan Plateau, Inner Mongolia, having a very signifi-

cant role in the ancient wars.

Now it ceased to be an important military post, but its unique disposition and design renders it important in the history of the building of the Great Wall.

Guyuan City （固原城）

It is an important town on the Great Wall, the location of Guyuan of the Ming Dynasty. It locates in the south of Ningxia Hui Nationality Autonomous Region. To its east lies Pengyang; to its southeast, Pingliang City, Gansu; to its south, Longde and Jingyuan; to its north, Tongxin; and to its west, Haiyuan and Xiji. Since the ancient times, Guyuan has been an important town in the northwest, a hub on the northern road of the eastern segment of the Silk Road. In the Spring and Autumn Period and the Warring States Period, tribes such as Yiqu and Wusirong were active there. State Qin set up Beidi County there. After Qin's unification of China, it set up Wusi County to the south of today's city site. In the third year of Yuanding of Emperor Wu of the Western Han

Dynasty (114 BC) Anding Magistrate was set up to manage Gaoping County, today's Guyuan City. In the beginning years of the Ming Dynasty, Guyuanwei was established, and then changed to Guyuan Magistrate, under the administration of Pingliangfu, Shaanxi. In the years of Chenghua of Emperor Xianzong, a combined local government was set up to control the military affairs of three towns, Yulin, Ningxia and Gansu. In the fourteenth year of Hongzhi (1501), Guyuan Town was set up, being one of the nine frontier cities.

In the third year of Wanli (1575), governor Shi Maozu led his soldiers and civilians to build a brick-covered wall. Due to its position at the throat of Liupan, it acquired the name of the No.1 city of Gaoping. It is a strategically important place for military leaders of various times. Now the northwestern corner still exists.

Ancient Wuwei City （武威古城）

It lies in the middle of Wuwei area, Gansu. It acquired its name because of the Han troops expedition to Hexi. The name literally means military strength. As early as in the Han and Tang dynasties, it was an important military and political city in the Hexi area as well as the economic and cultural center. It is the largest ancient city in northwestern

China, second only to Chang'an. In the Tang Dynasty, to ward off the Tubos and Turks, a military post was appointed in Hexi area, with its office located at Wuwei.

After the establishment of the Ming Dynasty, in the ninth year of Hongwu (1376), Liangzhouwei was set up there. In the tenth year of Hongwu (1377), a military commander called Pu Ying added a 3-*chi* wall to the original one, making it 5 *zhang* and 1 *chi* in height. The city has eastern, southern, and northern gates. In the twenty-fourth year of Hongwu, the military commander Song Sheng added a western gate and built three gate towers on the southern, eastern, and northern gate. A moat of 2 *zhang* in depth and 3 *zhang* in width was also dug. Drawbridges were used for access. Surrounding the

city wall 56 arrow turrets were built. To the west of the northern city a high tower was built that could observe a range of tens of miles. By then, Wuwei became the eastern gate of the Hexi Passageway as a complete, independent defense system.

Ancient Zhangye City　(张掖古城)

It locates in the central and northern parts of Zhangye area, Gansu Province, an important town on the Silk Road. In the Han Dynasty, Sude County was set up. In the Jin Dynasty, Yongping County was set up there. In the Sui Dynasty, it was changed to Zhangye County. In the Tang Dynasty, it was called Ganzhou. After the Tang Dynasty, it was controlled by the Tubos. It belonged to Western Xia in the Song Dynasty. In the Ming Dynasty, Zhangye was called Ganzhouwei, the very western town of the nine towns on the Great Wall. It was also the site of Gansu Town. The present Zhangye City has a circumference of over 6 kilometers. In the years of Wanli of the Ming Dynasty, the wall was covered with bricks.

As an ancient city with a long history, Zhangye has rich cultural heritage. There were many temples in the ancient times in Zhangye. There was once a saying, half the city is under the shades of pagodas. Among its numerous historical sites, the Dafo (Great Buddha) Temple is the most famous.

Ancient Jiuquan City　(酒泉古城)

It locates in the southeast of Jiuquan area, Gansu. According to legends, the Golden Spring there was where the famous Western Han general, Huo Qubing, got his wine, hence the name, literally meaning wine spring.

In the Han Dynasty, it was called Fulu County. It changed to Jiuquan County in the Sui Dynasty. After the middle period of the Tang Dynasty, it belonged to the Tubos. In the twenty-ninth year of Hongwu of the Ming Dynasty (1396), when Jiuquan City was expanding, this city gate was changed into a drum tower, i.e. today's Jiuquan Drum Tower. In the Ming Dynasty, Suzhouwei was set up in Jiuquan. When Feng Sheng conquered Qigua and Shazhou outside the Great Wall, Suzhou was the No.1 northwestern frontier town.

The famous historical sites of Jiuquan include Neolithic remains, Han and Tang tombs, Han, Tang, Yuan and Ming architectures, etc. They are of high calibre, with 25 of them being key national cultural relics protection units.

Jiayuguan Pass （嘉峪关）

It is also called Great Pass of the World, locating to the west of Jiayuguan City, Gansu Province. It lies at the hub of the Hexi Passageway, with Wenshu Mountain of the Qilian Ridges to its south and the endless Hei Mountain to its north. The pass was

located on Jiayuyuan between the two mountains, and coupled with the crossing the Taolai River, its geographic position is extremely critical. It is the best-preserved pass among hundreds of passes of the Great Wall.

In the fifth year of Hongwu of the Ming Dynasty (1372), the Ming general, Feng Sheng, led his men to march into Hexi area. After taking the area, he thought that with rivers and mountains, Jiayuguan was an ideal place for building a pass. He therefore made suggestions to the court to abandon guarding Dunhuang and to build the Jiayuguan Pass.

The inner city of the pass lies at the center of the pass. The plan of the pass is a trapezium in shape, with the western side bigger than the eastern side. The eastern wall has a length of 154 meters; the western wall, 166 meters; and the southern and northern walls, 160 meters. The wall has a height of 9 meters. If the arrow-loops are added the height is 10.7 meters. 6 meters of the wall from the ground is built with rammed loess, while the part above it is built with earth adobes. The city, except for gates, horse faces, watchtowers, arrow-loops, keeps, etc. is built with bricks as exterior. The inner city has two gates, namely, eastern and western gates. The eastern gate is called Guanghua, and the western one Rouyuan. On top of each of the two gates a tower was built, with green tiles and red railings and heavily decorated beams and columns. These towers were built by Li Duancheng in the Ming Dynasty. The towers are 13 meters in height, divided into three stories that are wooden saddleback structures with three eaves. On the ridges of the towers many animal sculptures were added that vividly enhance the decoration of the buildings. On the four corners of the pass city corner horse faces were built, with corner turrets on them. From afar, the whole pass city is magnificent with its many towers and castles.

In the past decades, many places of the Jiayuguan Pass have been repaired. In 1961, it was listed by the State Council as key national cultural relics protection units. Now the pass attracts more and more visitors.

Jiayuguan Pass

嘉峪关

Xuanbi Great Wall （悬壁长城）

It lies to the west of the Huangcaoying Village, Jiayuguan Town, 7.5 kilometers north of Jiayuguan Pass, on the eastern slope of Hei Mountain to the north of Shiguan Gorge. It is the northern end of the Suzhou Western Great Wall, built in the nineteenth year of Jiajing of the Ming Dynasty (1540) by a military commander, Li Han. The original length of 1.5 kilometer is made of stone slabs and rammed earth. The remaining segment today has a base width of 4 meters, a top width of 4 meters, and various heights ranging from 0.5 to 6 meters. The stone slab layers are 10 to 15 centimeters in thickness, while the earth layer has a thickness of 10 to 13 centimeters. The segment of rammed loess wall on the waist of the mountain has a width of 48 centimeters and a height of 30 centimeters. In 1987, it was rebuilt, with a length of 500 meters, among which 231 meters was built on mountain slope, with a base width of 4 meters, a top width of 2 meters, and a height of 6 meters. The thickness of the stone slab layer and the earth layers are similar to the previous one. Arrow-loops and a special wall structure were added on top of the wall, with a horse face on each end of it. A horse walk in the forms of steps was built on the mountain slope and the first horse face. When ascending the steps, visitors will feel like walking on plain or climbing a cliff. Because there is a segment of the Great Wall that was built on a ridge that has a height of 150 meters and an inclination of 45 degrees, therefore modern people named it Xuanbi, meaning suspended wall.

Yumenguan Pass （玉门关）

Yumenguan was one of the gateways to the West in the Western Han Dynasty as well as an important pass on the Han Great Wall. The southern and northern routes of the Silk Road have to pass through Yumenguan. It is said that the high quality jade from Hetian in the West was transported from Tarim Basin through this pass, hence the name, meaning "gate of jade". It was set up in the third year of Yuanfeng of Emperor Wu of the Han Dynasty and witnessed three prosperities and three abandonments. In 1944, Xia Nai and Yan Wenru from the former Northwest Science Investigation Team History Group conducted an excavation at the Han Great Wall fire signal tower remains at Xiaofangpan City and its eastern side. They concluded that the Han Yumenguan was in the site of Xiaofangpan City, northwest of Dunhuang County, 90 kilometers away from the county. The city is square in shape, with relatively complete walls that are made of rammed loess.

In 1979, Gansu Museum's Cultural Relics Team and Dunhuang County Cultural Institute formed a joint Han Great Wall Investigation Team. Taking into account their findings of the Great Wall, they further located the site of Yumenguan as to the west of Majuan Bay. However, no acceptable conclusion is reached so far as to the actual site of Yumenguan.

Yangguan Pass （阳关）

Like Yumenguan, it is also an important pass on the Han Great Wall. Also, it was a hub through which the southern and northern routes of the Silk Road must pass. According to historical records, Yangguan lied to the south of Yumenguan. South is yang in Chinese, while north is yin, hence the name, meaning southern pass literally.

Yangguan has been the object of praise by many Chinese poets in the history, especially the most famous *Wei City Ode* by the great Tang poet, Wang Wei. But where is it? In 1972, when a cultural relics census was conducted in Jiuquan area, the archaeologists crossed fourteen sand ridges westwards from Gudongtan and finally found a remaining city site in the desolated desert. The city has an area of over 10,000 square meters. Many Han coins, arrowheads, earthware shards, arable lands, kilns, and channels were also discovered. The archaeologists tentatively believed that it was the site of the ancient Yangguan.

Interior of a watchtower at Jinshan Ridge Great Wall
金山岭长城敌楼内景

Appendix 2 :

Architectures of the Great Wall

Brick wall
砖 砌 墙

The brick structure's large-scale adoption began in the Ming Dynasty. The present brick Great Wall was also built in that dynasty. The main body of the Ming brick Great Wall is divided into foundation, wall and arrow-loops.

Stone slabs were the most often used foundation material, with uniform wall bricks laid on top of it. The outer and inner sides and the top of the wall were laid with bricks, while inside the wall broken bricks, pebbles, and loess were added and rammed solidly. The section of the wall is trapezium in shape, with the top smaller than the base. The brickwork adopted joints technique in each layer of bricks to increase the strength internally. The foundation of the wall generally has a depth of 2 to 5 meters, 1 to 2 meters thicker than the wall in order to secure the firmness of the wall. A special mortar was used on the top and the outer and inner sides of the wall, which was made of lime and rice juice or plant oil. The adhesion of this mortar is very durable. The top of the wall was covered with brick floor, with arrow-loops added and water gutter designed.

The wall brickwork has three categories, cross, plum blossom, and three-seven. Plum blossom style is the most often used in the Ming Great Wall construction.

Stone wall
石 砌 墙

The employment of stones in buildings or structures has a long history in China. For instance, many walls of the pre-Qin Great Wall are made of stones. After the Qin and Han dynasties, stone structure had a great development.

In the building of the Ming Great Wall, many stone materials and structures were used, with some segments built entirely with stone materials. The stone used is rubble (without working or slightly worked, irregular in shape) or slabs (also irregular in shape, but has two parallel sides). The rubble wall generally tried to make the exterior side of the wall even, and then mortar was used to seal the interstices. The slabs were worked slightly. The wall interstices are not regular but horizontal interstices are obvious. Some walls adopted rubble or slabs in building the main body, while bricks were used to build arrow-loops and other structures on top of the wall. Some walls were built with regular slabs on two sides, with rubble rammed in between. The top of the wall was covered with 3 to 4 bricks. The surface was built with horse walk with square bricks and the arrow-loops and other top structures were also made of bricks.

Ramming-earth wall
夯 土 墙

Ramming-earth wall is the earliest method adopted by China to construct a wall, using layered ramming earth to build a wall. Loess with no impurities was commonly used in Loess Plateau, while for other areas clay was more popular. Planks were used as molds in which clay or lime was filled, and then rammed with pestles.

Along the Great Wall, there are many ramming-earth walls. Some of them are of clay and sand, adding wicker or reed in ramming. Other use earth, sand, lime and gravel in ramming. The height of such walls is generally two times the thickness of their bases, with the width of their tops a quarter or one fifth of the height, therefore, the wall has apparent shuttle shape. The wall so constructed has some bearing strength, impeding the advance of the enemy infantry and cavalry and resisting the cold arms (knife, lance, arrow, etc.) attack. It can utilizes nearby materials therefore is less demanding in engineering. Therefore, before the Sui Dynasty, this kind of walls was common. In the Han Dynasty, the ramming earth layer was around 15 centimeters. Thanks to the progress in construction, the lay in Tang and Ming dynasties was around 30 centimeters.

Adobe wall
土 坯 墙

Adobe wall uses adobes in construction. Clay was made into adobe. When dried, these adobes were cemented by clay just as in bricklaying to make a wall. The exterior would be covered by a coat of loess as protection. Although bricks and adobes both use clay as raw material, straw can be added in adobes to make it safe from cracking. The wall at Jiayuguan Pass is mostly made of such adobes. The bearing strength and role of this kind of walls are similar to that of the ramming-earth ones. It also utilized nearby resources, but more convenient than ramming earth. Furthermore, it does not need shuttle shape to make high walls. For example, the wall at Jiayuguan Pass reaches as high as 9 meters. This kind of wall suits areas with little precipitation and dry weather. It is easier for the enemy to destroy and not resistant to long weathering.

In laying method, it differs from brick walls: the bricks in brick wall are laid flat with their longest dimensions perpendicular to the face of the wall, with three or five bricks forming a course; while for adobe wall, the adobes are laid standing on their ends, generally, one layer of standing adobes with a layer of flat ones, and no mortar on sides, either, only between faces. Thus, due to the wall's own gravitational pressure, it can stand weight. If laid flat, owing to its coarseness in making, it may break.

Cliff wall
削 险 墙

In constructing the Great Wall, when a precipitous cliff was in the way it was used as a wall and the keeps were built on top of it; or such a cliff was made manually to serve as a wall; or using a natural cliff directly as a part of the Great Wall and continued the construction from the other side of the mountain, thus leaving the natural obstacle without any wall. This kind of using natural topography in building the Great Wall is called cliff wall.

Corner tower
角 楼

It was built on the corners of the city wall, generally in the shape of square or circular protruding from the wall. Its function is similar to a gate tower. The earliest record of it appeared in *Crafts* of *Zhou Li (Rites of Zhou)* in the Zhou Dynasty. It was at that time called Yu, meaning corner in Chinese, which was 2 *zhang* higher than the wall. The physical evidence also first appeared on the Han frontier walls, such as on the four corners of the ancient Chaolukulun City in Chaoge County, Inner Mongolia. They are protruding with an inclination of 45 degrees, with a top area of 5 × 5 meters and regular forms. Similar structures can be found in other segments of the frontier walls.

On many passes of the Ming Great Wall corner towers were also built, such as Shanhaiguan and Jiayuguan passes.

Wall terrace
墙 台

On the Great Wall, there is a protrusion every certain distance called wall terrace or horse face.

The advent of horse face gave the defending soldiers good view of the field. It also facilitated flexible tactics on battling on the wall, initiating a three-dimensional battlefield and breaking the former horizontal fighting disposition. Its benefit includes protruding but not crossing, with arrow-loops at both sides throwing rocks and launching arrows. The distance between two such terraces is roughly 40 *zhang*, forming a three-dimensional fire net and greatly enhancing the fighting and defending functions of the wall.

Watchtower
敌 台

The watchtower was built on the wall, protruding outwards in order to counterattack the offensive. It was a tall tower, also called enemy tower. In Northern Song Dynasty Zeng Gongliang described in *Wu Jing Zong Yao (Compendium of Martial Arts)* that it was built on horse face and build with wood structures. Every side has one room two columns or three rooms four columns; the three outward sides were paneled with planks and designed with arrow loops; wood beams were added to its top to make a flat cover; on top of this cover thick earth was laid to protect it from stone and arrow attack; some parts were covered with cow hide to resist fire rocket. The enemy keeps on Ming Great Wall were built crossing the wall normally, called hollow keeps. This type was created by Qi Jiguang, a famous Ming general, when he was in charge of building the Jizheng part of the Great Wall. These keeps consist normally of upper, middle, and lower parts. The lower part is a base, constructed by large slates, with a similar height to the wall. The middle part is hollow, some of which are built with bricks or brick arches, connecting them into narrow rooms; others with wood pillars and wooden floors covered by thick and heavy brick walls to make one or two stories of inner space for soldiers, food and fodder, and arms.

The Ming watchtowers sometimes were independent of the wall and sometimes without arrow windows but only access to the top, actually a solid watchtower. This kind is most found on the Xuanfu and Datong Great Walls.

Inner wall and arrow-loops
女墙、垛口

The inner wall refers to the shorter wall on top of the Great Wall, generally built on the inner side like a railing. On some of the inner wall of the Ming Great Wall, arrow-loops were designed too.

Arrow-loops are built on city walls or defense works, in the form of alternating high and low structures. On the outer wall of the Great Wall and the top of the watchtowers, arrow-loops are built.

The arrow-loop was used to observe the enemy and cover the archers. When the wall was laid to the height of waist from the wall floor, arrow-loops began to appear. They are rectangular in shape, generally. There is a square hole on the upper part of them for watching. Special brickwork is used for convenience of observing the enemy and for protecting the observer. In the lower part, another square hole is designed for shooting arrows. The lower side of the hole inclined downwards in order to shoot the enemy below.

Barrier wall
障 墙

It was built on the horse walk of the wall, alongside the steps and perpendicular to the arrow-loops on the wall. The thin barrier wall is unique to the Jizhen Great Wall. When the Great Wall was built on very steep slopes, the soldiers would

be easily exposed to the enemy weapons. Therefore, a short wall that is perpendicular to the arrow-loops was designed on the inner side of the arrow-loops. The height of barrier walls is similar to arrow-loop walls, with watch holes and shooting holes. Due to the steep slope, the arrow-loop walls and inner walls were designed into dentation walls, leaving a narrow passageway for a single soldier. On the Jinshan Ridge and Simatai Great Walls, the barrier walls are imposing and inclined to the valley, obviously for the purpose of defending against the enemy who had invaded into the inner side of the wall.

Rock hole
礌石孔

It was used to let go rolling logs and rocks to attack the invading enemy, generally designed at the lower part of the arrow-loop walls. There are some such structures on some segments of the Jizhen Great Wall.

Take Simatai Great Wall as an example. The rock holes of the Simatai Great Wall have an inner width and height of about 50 centimeters, with complex brickworks. The lower half of the inner hole is square pre-set hole, while the upper half is built into archway shape with irregular bricks. On top of its outer hole a stone cap is used for cover, which was made into semicircular shape on the inner side. The outer side protrudes from the wall like eaves. Below the outer hole, circular grooves are built with irregular bricks, be it stone-walls or brick walls. The length of the grooves varies in different segments, from 85 centimeters to 2 meters, all designed into a shape that features greater depth of the upper part and smaller depth of the lower part, with a smooth gradient.

Horse walk
马道

It refers to the road on the Great Wall that were designed for horses or riding horses, generally referred to the wall floor on the top of the Great Wall. It was used by the defense forces to dispose in the whole city. When war came, the soldiers and horses could move quickly under the cover of the Great Wall, saving time and securing safety.

Where the mountain slope is too steep, there are two methods of building horse walks. One is like building heaven ladder, meaning to divide the horse walk into inner and outer parts. The outer side was built with special structures for the soldiers to guard, while the inner side was built into passageway for moving soldiers. The other method builds the horse walk entirely into passageway.

Where it connects with the hollow watchtowers, there are three methods for adjusting the difference of the heights. When the gate of the watchtower far exceeds the horse walk in height, the walk would be built into an ascending passageway or heaven ladder. When the gate of the watchtower is much lower compared with that of the horse walk, the wall either directly connects with the upper story of the watchtower and uses other access for the gate of the watchtower, or makes the center of the wall a descending passageway, with both sides arrow-loops and inner walls maintaining their original heights but the outer eave wall was built thicker than the inner eave wall. When the gate of the watchtower is similar to the horse walk, the treatment is simply adding a passageway on the walk.

City access
登城道

It is generally designed on the inner side of the wall, for generals and soldiers to gain access to the wall. It is generally a single slope, with floor, but sometimes, a railing wall was added on the outer side. Most of such structures were built near watchtowers, while a few were built between two watchtowers.

On some segments of the wall, the inside elevation is similar to the height of the horse walk. In such cases, no separate access was used, but an opening or an archway was used on the inner wall of the Great Wall.

Pass blockade
关口障碍

It was used to strengthen the defense of the passes. The passes on the Great Wall are generally designed at valleys or road junctions in order to control important passageways. Therefore, besides building the passes and castles, the establishment of blockade was also stressed. Outside the Great Wall, the mountain slopes were cut into steep cliffs in order to make it difficult for the enemy riders to approach. On even grounds, big pits in small triangle groups were dug with iron bars and knives at the bottom. In front of the pits thick low bushes were planted to hinder the movement of the enemy and to provide cover to the blockade. Some soldiers were sent in ambush or as bait to trap the enemy into the pits, or they would block the enemy advancement or sabotage.

Single-sided wall

单边墙

It is a custom name given by the local people alongside the Jizhen Great Wall. The difference between it and common wall is that it consists of only one thin wall. It is built on top of steep, high summits or ridges, where no soldier or horse can possibly access the outer side of it. It is an expedient way of building wall.

It was built with unworked large rubbles, with coarse mortar as adhesive. The height and thickness of it varies according to topography.

There are three segments of the Simatai Great Wall that adopt single-sided wall, with varying structures and methods. The first segment is brick wall, an arrow-loop wall with barrier wall on the slope. The second is less than 100 meters in length, with some space on the inner side for soldiers. Two rows of shooting holes were built on top of it. The third lies between Xiannu Tower and Wangjing Tower, with a length of 300 meters, on extremely ridges. On both the inner and outer sides of the wall there is no room for soldiers and horses, therefore there is no arrow-loop on the wall. The last two segments were built with large rubbles.

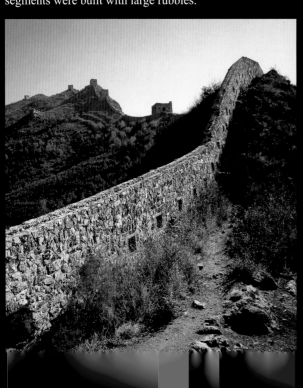

Gate and passageway

门 和 通 道

The gates and passageways of the Great Wall were generally designed cleverly. The gate refers to the opening on different parts of the Great Wall for military personnel to enter and exit, called archway gate. The passageway refers to the traffic route between pass, watchtower, fighting terrace, and the main body of the wall. Some of them were designed on the inner side of the wall, not on top of it. The gates and passageways mentioned here do not include the large and small gates for carriages and horse to enter and exit the pass. A Bianmen, i.e. archway gate, locates on the inner side of the Great Wall, the passageway for guarding forces to ascend and descend the wall and watchtowers, but cannot be used to reach the northern city. The gate was built on the inner side of the Great Wall, in the form of an arch, with a height of 2 meters or so, a width of 60 to 80 centimeters, and a depth of about 1.5 meters. The upper part of it is in the shape of an arch, then perpendicular to the main body of the wall more than ten steps were built upwards. At the end of the steps, another arch was built for the sakes of safety and waterproof. The Bianmens at Gubeikou and Jielingkou have left and right openings, with ascending steps for horse walk. Wooden doors were assembled outside, and this kind of Bianmens was used for soldiers to obtain firewood, food and fodder, and other supplies. Besides Bianmen, on the two inner sides of pass gate Bianmens were also designed, with steps to the main body of the wall on the two sides.

Dry pass

旱 关

At a pass of the Great Wall, the parts connected with the Great Wall but form a closed city called pass city. Because there is no river passing the city area, therefore it is called dry pass. Dry passes are bigger than city barriers, with more troops stationed and more food, fodder, and other supplies stored there. In attacking, it served as the gate of the advancing troops, while in defending, it closed the route to the pass. Its shape is not fixed, but varying according to the topography and defense requirements at the pass. On even plains, it is mostly square or rectangular in shape, such as Shanhaiguan Pass and Jiayuguan Pass; on mountainous areas, the shape adapts to the surrounding topography. For example, the pass city of Gubeikou is between two mountains. In accordance with the size and topography of the pass city, there are generally two to four gates.

The gates are the access to the pass city in peaceful times while in war times, it will be used as the exit for the attacking soldiers. In early times, wooden beams were used. After the Yuan Dynasty, brick or stone archways were adopted. Giant double wooden doors were equipped in the archway. The wooden doors were covered with iron sheet and consolidated with big pikes. Latch and rings were added to the inner side of the doors. Some were even built with special devices to attack the invading enemy forces. To strengthen the firmness, the steps near the gate mostly adopted stone slabs in construction. Many gates were decorated with tablets showing their names. In most cases, the gates are dry gates for land traffic.

Water pass
水 关

It was used when the Great Wall met rivers or valleys. Its purpose was to not hinder the passage of the water while using the topography as a means of defense.

It is a building in the form of bridge arch, with arrow-loops built on the top and arches for the running water. Its facilities can be divided into two categories: land facilities, including wall, gun turrets, land gates, barracks, command office, corner towers, etc; water facilities, including breakwaters, water gates, sluice gates, dam sills, etc. The two sets of facilities are interdependent. The large water passes on the Ming Great Wall include Jiumenkou, Huangyaguan Water Pass; the smaller ones include Qingshanguan Pass in Qianxi County, Hebei Province.

Archway and gateway
拱券及城门洞

The early gateways of the passes used linking beam in construction. Along with the development of construction technology and the vast adoption of bricks, the gateway began to use brick and stone materials in construction. Generally, rectangular slabs were used as foundation, then three to five layers of rectangular slabs were used for base, with a height of 1 to 1.5 meters. Then horizontal bricks were used for the top. When the design requirements are met, vertical and horizontal bricks would be used according to the structure. In the brick and stone structure, the spanning structure utilizing the building block's sideway pressure is called arch.

In the Ming brick Great Wall, besides the adoption of brick arches in the gates and water gateways, most watchtowers also used such structures. The arrow windows and gateways of the watchtowers cannot do without brick or stone arches. The barracks of the watchtowers sometimes also used arches covered with tiles, making them entire brick structures.

The relatively large arches along the Great Wall include Juyongguan Pass, Bada Ridge Great Wall, Zijingguan Water Gate, etc. Rectangular stone tablets are set on the arches, with the passes names on them. Some decorations built with bricks or stones were also added to the arches. Two wooden doors were assembled in the gateway, covered with iron sheet, preventing the enemy's entrance from the gates.

Pass tower
关 楼

It is also called city tower or gate tower. It was a city's public building in peaceful times, while in war times, it became the command office of the key generals. Although it was not built in the front line of fighting, the military functions are obvious. It served as observation and command post, as well as a fighting unit.

The tower is generally wooden or brick and wooden structure of one, two, or three stories, with hip roof, overhang gabled roof, or gable-hip roof. Bucket arch was generally used in these structures. The entire building was usually decorated with paint on both the interior and exterior. By so doing, the whole tower not only has artistic value and serious look, but also provides military function and aesthetic enjoyment. The No.1 Pass in the world tower of Shanhaiguan Pass is such as gable-hip roof structure of two stories. The two three-story towers on top of Guanghua Gate and Rouyuan Gate of the Jiayuguan Pass are painted with an orange color by the sun. The green glazed tiles on the gable and hip roof are shining and the animal-shaped tiles, dragons, lions, etc. on the ridges become more vividly.

Wengcheng
瓮 城

To prevent the direct exposure of the city gate to the enemy, extra walls were added at the gate area to form a small defense structure, called Wengcheng. The name in Chinese means an urn-shaped city, meaning that when the enemy entered such structure they would be like a turtle in an urn.

It has two shapes, rectangular and semicircular. Its walls are generally shorter than that of the pass city, and thinner. Its openings are mostly on the side, connected with the main city gate with bent passageways for better defense. The opening on Wengcheng is called Weng gate. Major pass gates on the Great Wall such as that of the Shanhaiguan Pass and Jiayuguan Pass were all added with Wengcheng. Originally, all the four gates of Shanhaiguan were built withWengcheng, but now only the Wengcheng of the eastern gate is remaining. The two Wengchengs of the two gates of Jiayuguan are still seen today.

Luocheng
罗 城

It is extra circular wall added to the city wall for the purpose of strengthening the defense of the city wall. Such structures were used in the pass cities of Shanhaiguan and Jiayuguan. Originally, there were eastern and western Luocheng at Shanhaiguan, outside the eastern and western gates of the pass. Now only the eastern Luocheng is remaining. There is Luocheng outside the Rouyuan Gate of Jiayuguan Pass, with a gate facing the west. It is the official gate of the pass, with a stone tablet reading Jiayuguan Pass. There was a tower on top of the gate, but now demolished.

Luocheng is a " Ⅱ "shape wall structure outside Wengcheng in the direction of the expected enemy attack. The Luocheng is relatively long, not only providing protection to Wengcheng, but also covering a long part of the inner city wall. It is the first defense line of the pass, making the defense more effective by increasing the depth of defense. Precious time could be gained by such depth of defense. On top of the wall of Luocheng, towers were generally built for observation of the enemy and for military command purposes. At the two ends of the city wall, ar-

City barrier
城 障

It is a small city built at difficult areas of the Great Wall for stationed troops. In the Qin and Han dynasties, along the Great Wall many small castles were built for the purpose of defending against the Huns, and they were sometimes called barriers. Several such small castles are found at Bayinnuoluo, Suhai, etc., Inner Mongolia. The cities are similar in size and form. The plane is square shape, with protruding wall terraces at the four corners.

The difference between a city and a city barrier is: besides military forces, there were civilians in a city, while in a city barrier, there were only servicemen.

row towers were designed generally to strengthen the watch and patrol. The Luocheng and inner city of Jiayuguan form a double-wall, facing the front line of the enemy attack.

Fire signal tower
烽火台

It is also called Fengsui. Setting fire called Feng (at night), and setting smoke called Sui (in daytime), meaning: when the enemy came in daytime, smoke would be made, and at night fire would be set up. The fire and smoke are all signals for sending alert to inner land and surrounding areas.

Fire signal towers had been integrated with the Great Wall after the Qin and Han Periods, forming an important part of the Great Wall defense. The disposition of fire signal towers along the Great Wall took into account of the local conditions. Some were built outside the frontier wall and extended outwards in order to detect the move of the enemy. Others were built inside the frontier wall and connected with passes and towns for the convenience of organizing effective counterattack. Still others were built along the two sides of the Great Wall, closely attached to the wall itself, for the purpose of quickly disposing the troops to fight the enemy.

In the meantime of setting up fire and smoke signals, the Ming Dynasty also used gun to send military signal. According to an official order in the second year of Chenghua of Emperor Xianzong (1466): the frontier towers are required to make fire or fire gun to send signal; if the enemy number ranges from a few up to one hundred, one fire and one gunshot will be used; if five hundred enemy come, two fires and two gunshots; over one thousand enemy, three fires and three gunshots; over five thousand, four fires and four gunshots; and over ten thousands, five fires and five gunshots.

Barrack castle
营 堡

It was used to station troops for observing the enemy, mostly built between two mountains or other difficult areas along the both sides of the frontier walls. Inside the Great Wall, there are many such barrack castles. Generally, within 1 to 1.5 kilometers inside the Great Wall gates there would be built with a barrack castle with firm structure for the purpose of making shifts with the Great Wall troops. It has two to four gates. The land inside such castle is even. Outside it there are often arable lands for the food supply.

The Ming barrack castle was often connected with passes. For example, a new and an old barrack castles were built at Shahukou, Youyu County, Shanxi Province, which is close to the Inner Mongolia. The new castle was for civilians to live in. Businessmen and traders were resided both inside and outside the new castle; while the old castle stationed troops. The old castle has only one southern gate, while the new castle has two gates, the southern and the northern gates, which are connected with the old castle to form a triple-gate to three gates on a south-north line. Walls were built to connect the two castles to form a single bigger castle, with eastern and western gates. The road connecting Inner Mongolia and Shanxi Province passes through the eastern and the western gates.

Brick kiln
砖 窑

When the Ming government built the Great Wall, the bricks, stones, mortar, and other materials were obtained or made from local areas. There are remains of brick kilns and mortar kilns in many villages along the Great Wall. For example, Qingquan Village, Qian'an County, Xiaozhangjiakou Village, Yanqing County, and the newly discovered Banchangyu, Funing County, Hebei Province.

The site of the kiln is very important in building such a kiln. General principles are: close to water, earth, firewood, city, and having good sunshine. The kilns are found in groups. By so doing, the production of bricks enjoyed convenient earth supply, water supply, firewood supply, good conditions for making adobes and drying and burning. Transportation would not become a problem, saving manpower, materials, and funds.

A kiln consists of front chamber, kiln gate, wind passage, fire chamber, kiln bed, and kiln wall. The discovery and sorting out of the kilns of the Great Wall provide us with rare, valuable physical materials in studying the brick technology of the Great Wall.

Lime earth
灰 土

Since the Ming Dynasty, when ramming the earth layers, a certain amount of lime earth that was powder-like was added to increase the compressive strength of the earth layer. The earth layer built with rammed lime and common earth is called lime earth. Each layer is called a pace. According the requirement of the Qing *Engineering Regulations*, each pace should be laid in a thickness of 7 *cun* when loose and 5 *cun* when rammed. (*cun* is ancient Chinese measurement.) The buildings were based on lime earth, generally. The prospecting findings show that the lime earth foundations of some important building of the Qing Dynasty usually have a lime earth layer of 20 paces. When brick-cover was adopted in building the Great Wall, the center of the wall usually used rammed lime earth to fill.

Mortar kiln
灰 窑

Its disposition was decided by the local rock quality and firewood supply on the one hand, and convenience for centralized manpower in transportation, on the other. In investigation, it is found that mortar kilns are within vicinity of brick kilns generally. The several areas where such kilns are found to be densely disposed are Dalingzhai, Xichengyu, Dongjiakou, Qingquan, etc. where brick kilns have already been discovered in large numbers.

So far the investigated mortar kilns are not generally on the ground surface, in bad conditions, and with small sizes. In Dalingzhai larger and better-preserved mortar kiln remains were discovered, with the limestone mortar like newly burnt, except for the ineffectiveness of the mortar due to time elapse. However, the study of the disposition of the mortar kilns is not complete without further work done by the archaeologist workers in the future.

Moat
护 城 河

Digging deep ditches to replace city wall in suitable areas was common practice for building ancient Chinese cities. It is formed when digging for earth. Later, water was introduced to form another defense line around the city. Outside Shanhaiguan Pass there is a moat with a depth of about 2 *zhang* and a width of 5 *zhang*. The enemy had to wade through it to approach the city, adding to their difficulty in attacking and providing good opportunity for defensive forces to kill the enemy.

Some moats were dug manually, while others were made utilizing natural channels. The distance between the moat and the wall is generally tens of meters, sometimes as wide as 100 or 200 meters. As a city's surrounding defense work, the high walls and deep ditches form the main body of the defense system. Integrating the protection of the moats into that of the city wall is necessary. In some rare cases, lakes or large rivers were also used for moats.

Loulu
楼 橹

It is the terrace for watching the enemy move in the ancient times. In Qi Jiguang's *Lian Bing Shi Ji (Drilling Records)* of the Ming Dynasty, he wrote: when building hollow watchtowers on the Great Wall, Loulu should be built on top with surrounding arrow-loops. He referred to the buildings on top of a terrace for sheltering sentry soldiers. It is also called watch pavilion, watchtower, or barrack room. It is mostly divided into one or three overhang gabled roof structure. Some Loulu are bigger, with surrounding corridor. Others are square in shape with pinnacles. From the existing evidence, these Loulu are supported by five-beam or seven-beam wood frames, sometimes brick wall, brick and stone arch, and other structures are used. The rooms are covered with plain tiles (unglazed tiles), with animal figures on the ridges. The front ridge generally has watching animal figures on it.

The horse faces of the Ming Dynasty sometimes also were built with Loulu, with a similar structure to that of the watchtowers, providing shelter to the stationed troops.

Tile
瓦 件

Tiles are important waterproof material for buildings. Its advent effectively solved the waterproof problem of buildings, beginning the production of earthware tiles in China. As to the materials, besides ordinary gray tiles and a small number of red tiles, there are also black tiles and glazed tiles. In the building of the Great Wall, tiles were mostly used on pass towers. The tiles can be divided into: glazed tiles with colorful glaze on the earthen blanks and plain tiles that were made of clay and with gray color. The two kinds of tiles have their own coding methods, sizes, and matching accessories and animal figures. The buildings on the Great Wall, such as gate tower, arrow tower, corner tower, and Loulu, are all covered with plain tiles. The tiles and the accessories discovered now are divided into panel tiles, cylinder tiles, eaves tiles, and water drips.

Great Wall bricks
长 城 砖

Using large stone material in buildings is quicker and firmer than using earth, but due to its small volume, lightness, convenience in transportation and usage, and faster laying process, bricks were universally used in building the Great Wall, greatly improved the efficiency.

The vast adoption of bricks in the Great Wall construction not only relates to the production level of the times, but also relates to the weaponry then. Before the Ming Dynasty, the rammed earth or stone laid walls were enough to deal with cold weaponry such as knife, lance, and arrows. By the Ming Dynasty, gunpowder had been used in war, various guns advent made the power of the weapons greater. Consequently, firmer bricks and stones were required in building the Great Wall.

The brick is ideal construction material for supporting vertical load. According to sample experiments, after hundreds of years of weathering and pressure, its compressive strength, water absorption, and anti-frozen property are similar to today's new bricks. Besides, for the convenience of construction, different shapes were made for different positions. Such as long bricks, square bricks, arrow-loop bricks, shooting hole bricks, watching tower bricks, flag staff bricks, gutter bricks, etc. In addition, on some important segments of the Great Wall the bricks were inscribed with characters. As many as sixteen kinds of character bricks are found in the walls of Shanhaiguan alone.

Fighting wall
战 墙

Such walls were mostly built on a favorite topography 40 or 50 meters in front of the main wall at important positions of the Great Wall. Some places were built with several such structures. For example, there are four fighting walls along Xiaozhangjiakou , Xihongshan , Sansi to the northwest of Beijing. It was built generally with bricks and stones. It forced the enemy to spread before they planned to, so that they could be destroyed before they approach the main body of the wall. It could also serve to divide the format of the enemy forces, providing opportunity for defensive forces to defeat the invading enemy.

Its form and size depended on topography. On even ground, it was built thicker and higher, with arrow-loops and inner walls. On steep slopes, it was built shorter, with a height of 2.5 meters. Its major feature is providing three kinds of shooting holes for standing, kneeling, and prone positions; the shooting hole has four sides of 0.3 meters each. The three rows of the three kinds of shooting holes were arranged into plum blossom format, providing posts for more soldiers in fighting. Meanwhile, such format increases the firepower and the killing rate.

Grades of the frontier walls
边 墙 等 级

The construction projects of the frontier walls were classified into three grades, according to the records of the tablets.

Grade one frontier walls were built mostly at important passes, such as Shanhaiguan, Xifengkou, Songpenglu, Jinshan Ridge, Gubeikou, Mutian Ravine, etc. It was built mostly with a mixture of brick and stone, with even stone slabs as foundation and the arrow-loops, horse walks, and inner walls covered with bricks.

Grade two frontier walls used stone slabs and bricks on the outer side of the wall, with brick-covered arrow-loops. The inner side of the wall adopted rubble wall that had a height similar to the horse walk, with brick inner walls. For example, such walls are found at Jiumenkou, Luowenyu, Qiangziluchengg, Hongshankou, etc.

Grade three frontier walls were built with local materials, generally. Often, rubble was used to build walls, without fixed forms and sizes. For example, the branch walls of Jinshan Rigde were entirely built with rubble and limestone mortar. Some were built on cliffs that provided natural barriers, such as the segment of the eastern Simatai Great Wall. Besides, most of the stonewalls at places such as Taipingzhai, Huangyaguan, are also very simple.

Inspection terrace
演 武 台

The Huanghuacheng inspection terrace, Beijing, and Jiumenkou inspection terrace, Funing County, Qinhuangdao, are circular, with steps for ascending and sand in front of them. The local people call them general appointment terrace. There is a stonewall in front of the terrace, with arrow targets. It is for the purpose of inspecting the troops. There are also layered square inspection terraces.

Tablet and stone carving
碑碣、石刻

The tablets and stone carvings found on the Great Wall roughly show the building history of the Great Wall in the Ming Dynasty. The troops sent by the Ming government to station the nine towns had two major tasks: one was to maintain the peace of the border areas, preventing the northern peoples from moving southwards; the other was to strengthen the building of the frontier walls, which was continuous and divided into spring and autumn shifts. Among all the found tablets and carvings on the Great Wall, the contents focused  on events such as the Commencement Tablet, Spring and Autumn Shifts of the Wanli Period, and repairing of the walls and watchtowers. In terms of periods, there are the thirty-fifth and the forty-fifth year of Jiajing (1556 and 1566), the fourth year of Longqing (1570), the fifth, eleventh, twelfth, twenty-fifth, twenty-ninth, thirty-first, forty-fourth, and forty-fifth year of Wanli (1577, 1583, 1584, 1597, 1601, 1603, 1616, and 1617), an unknown year of Tianqi, the tenth year of Chongzhen (1637), etc. Besides, some character bricks with rectangular stamps are found, most of which belong to the Wanli Period of the Ming Dynasty. Near passes some cliff carvings are found, with the content of praising the scenery of the local mountains and rivers, including various forms of poems. Some of them are carved with dates.

Laolongtou
老龙头

Imposing Great Wall
长城雄姿

Sketch Map of the Great Wall of China 万里长城位置示意图

敦煌
Dunhuang

嘉峪关
Jiayuguan Pass

武威
Wuwei

西宁
Xining

兰州
Lanzhou

中卫
Zhongwei

银川
Yinchuan

定边
Dingbian

西安
Xi'an

呼和浩特
Hohhot

偏关
Pianguan Pass

太原
Taiyuan

郑州
Zhengzhou

八达岭
Bada Ridge

北京
Beijing

石家庄
Shijiazhuang

天津
Tianjin

济南
Jinan

山海关
Shanhaiguan Pass

沈阳
Shenya

CHINA